THE
FORENSICS
HANDBOOK

THE FORENSICS

HANDBOOK

THE SECRETS OF
CRIME SCENE INVESTIGATION

PETE MOORE

www.eye-books.com

First published in Great
Britain 2004

Eye Books
51a Boscombe Road
London W12 9HT
www.eye-books.com

Conceived and produced by
Elwin Street Limited
79 St. John Street
London EC1M 4NR
www.elwinstreet.com

Editor: Debbie Foy
Designer: Simon Osborne
Illustrations: Richard
Burgess and William Ings
(27, 33)

10 9 8 7 6 5 4 3 2 1

A CIP catalogue record for
this book is available at the
British Library.

ISBN 1-9030-7035-X

Printed in Singapore

Picture Credits
The publishers would like
to thank the following for
permission to reproduce
images:
Alamy Ltd: 23, 29, 43, 85,
Courtesy of Dr Stephen
Koehler: 13 top, 13 bottom,
17, 30, 35, 63 both, 82, 93,
109, 113, 123
Corbis: 20, 57, 77 top, 155
Getty Images:
77 bottom, 153
National Human Genome
Research Institute: 99
Rex Features: 16, 69, 95,
138, 143
Science Photo Library Ltd:
12 top, 12 bottom, 13
middle, 45, 60, 64, 67, 72,
74, 79, 81, 87, 98, 100,
107, 111, 117, 127, 128,
130, 137, 140
TopFoto: 151

CONTENTS

INTRODUCTION

Forensic science has inspired thousands of detective novels and is a common thread in hundreds of cop shows on TV. Its more gruesome aspects are the stuff of nightmares, and in fiction forensics often allows detectives to make startling conclusions from conveniently placed scraps of evidence.

Real-life forensics is more complex than this, and the need for privacy means that it often occurs behind closed doors, or hidden inside rapidly erected tents and screens at the crime scene. This book lets you get behind these barriers for a close-up view of the forensic scientists at work. You will also discover that correctly analysing evidence can generate vast amounts of information. For example, bloodstains can reveal not only who the blood came from, but what sort of weapon was used.

Chapter by chapter this book lifts the lid on the techniques experts use to fight crime. Some of these methods, such as fingerprinting and firearms analysis, have long histories. Others, such as genetic fingerprinting and mass spectrometry, are more recent arrivals that place the power of twenty-first-century science in the hands of the law.

The term "forensic" simply means suitable for a court of law. In all cases, forensic science demands diligence and attention to detail if the work is going to bridge the gap from the crime scene to the courtroom. A criminalist (one who practises forensic science) should be able to decipher clues found on items of evidence and present them with sufficient clarity for a jury to understand the technique and trust the findings. Forensic science should lead investigators to the truth. Done well it should let innocent people walk free, but place criminals behind bars.

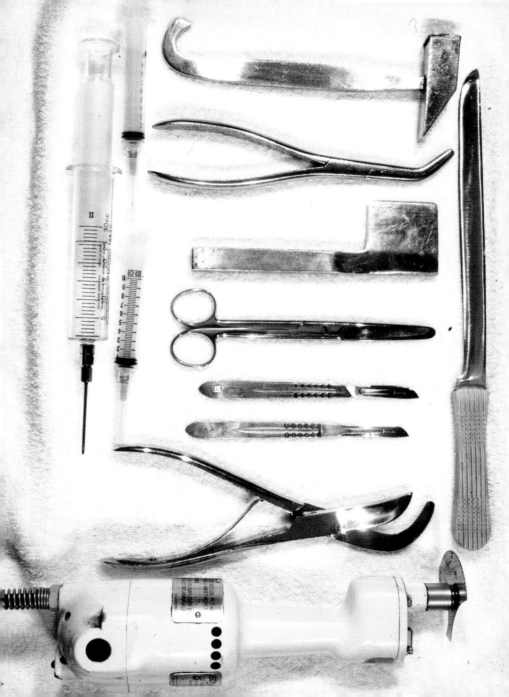

THE PROCESS

Section 1: page 8

- The Team • The Crime Scene
- Physical Evidence
- Scientific Analysis of Samples

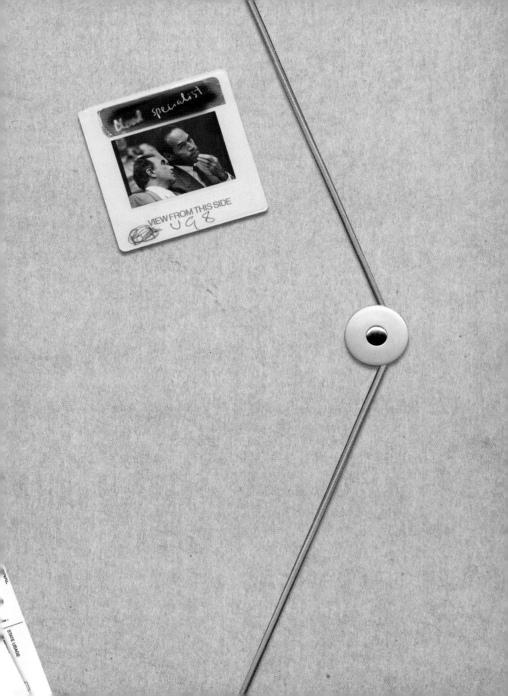

THE TEAM

At one time a criminalist may have covered a number of disciplines, and worked alone. These days, however, the typical forensic expert is a specialist who is part of a team. Criminals, after all, operate in every avenue of human endeavour, from building to banking, in corporate facilities or within homes. Consequently forensic science needs to reach into every corner of human activity, and use all available technologies and expertise. No one person can handle every area, and cooperation between disciplines is key. In general, the following principles apply to all forensic organisations.

HIERARCHY OF THE INVESTIGATION TEAM

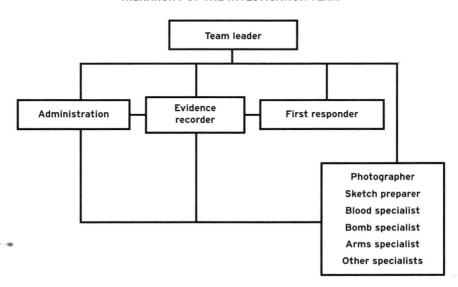

Manpower

The size of the forensics team varies, and on the whole the level of public concern about the crime gives a good guide to how large the team will be. While the theft of a bicycle may receive little police attention, the murder of a young girl or embezzlement from a large corporation can trigger massive investigations in which a senior police officer will coordinate the actions of hundreds of police and dozens of civilian forensic specialists.

Administration

There is no point staging a manhunt if you can't collate the data gathered or coordinate a plan of action, so good organisation and administration are vital parts of any investigation. In large incidents, the investigators are subdivided into small units, each of which is led by a head, who reports regularly to the senior investigator (see page 10).

Integrity of evidence

When the crime involves several distinct locations, a separate team deals with each place. This prevents one site being contaminated by material from another site. Even if the specialists are confident in their ability to avoid cross-contamination, the use of separate teams prevents defendants raising doubts about the validity of evidence by claiming in court that contamination could have occurred.

MANY SKILLS MAKE LIGHT WORK

The members of a forensic team have often trained in one particular science-based discipline, such as chemistry, medicine, pathology, psychology or photography, and then taken additional professional qualifications enabling them to apply these skills to law enforcement.

A FORENSICS ROLL CALL

Crime labs are often divided into a number of sections or units. The physical science unit takes techniques developed in chemistry, physics and geology and applies them to pieces of evidence. In a large laboratory, the physical science set-up may be subdivided into teams that specialise in individual materials, such as drugs, paints, explosives or soils.

Biology unit

This unit has a massive focus on analysing DNA, as this is a powerful marker that can link individuals with a crime, while exonerating other suspects. This unit also analyses plant samples and microscopic trace evidence, such as pollen or bacteria, that can give investigators vital clues in piecing together events surrounding a crime. A sub-section of the biology unit will focus solely on extracting information from blood.

Photographic unit

These specialists are called upon by other units to help record evidence before it is examined, as well as during its examination. Forensic photographers use specialised films and lighting to reveal information that the human eye can't see. Nowadays, these experts handle and analyse digital images, so that the forensic team can keep abreast of photographic counterfeiters.

Firearms unit

Ballistics experts are kept busy by the frequent misuse of guns. This unit has firing ranges for testing weapons, and microscopes for scrutinising bullets and shell cases. A unit may itself have equipment for analysing chemicals and gunpowder residues, or may outsource this to the physical science unit.

Document examination unit

This unit becomes involved in a huge range of crimes, from passport forgery to murder. These specialists draw on many different skills, including analysing the chemicals in ink and working out the sorts of marks that different printing techniques leave on paper.

Fingerprint unit

Crime novels love to concentrate on the fingerprint unit in a laboratory, although because criminals are well aware of the need to wear gloves this is not always the busiest section. Even so, many crimes are not carefully planned, in which case fingerprints can become valuable means of showing who's been present at a crime scene.

For example, a forensic computer expert could not assess how a computer has been used without years of previous experience in the computer industry. Indeed, investigators often subcontract people working in industry to help with specific specialised tasks. Other specialists, such as a firearms expert, can enter the profession after getting a college degree and receive on-the-job training.

THE FORENSICS LAB

Forensic science is a huge industry. Today there are literally hundreds of public crime laboratories to assist police at town, city and county level. However, there is no such thing as a standard forensics laboratory. Some large city-based labs are attached to universities or police departments. Others are independent agencies working for a range of clients, and may employ dozens of people, all working in particular specialities. By contrast, a laboratory that serves a small town may be run by a single scientist and packed with numerous pieces of equipment. The scientist sends off pieces of evidence to specialist consultants, effectively creating his or her own team.

A forensics laboratory looks drab and uninspiring: white-boxed lumps of technology stand on a scrupulously clean floor or sit on benchtops bereft of personal touches. The excitement lies in the lab workers' ability to combine machines, skills and experience to glean valuable data from the most unpromising samples. Large or small, every forensic lab needs to implement the following two standard procedures:

1. The contamination of samples must be avoided. If a blood smear found at a crime scene and a blood sample taken from a suspect somehow come into contact with one another, any findings are of no forensic value,

so a laboratory needs to run management systems that ensure such an event can never happen. If evidence is documented, collected and stored in the correct manner, it can often be presented in court several years after the ciminal act took place.

2. Every lab must have a rigorous method of recording evidence, including keeping track of who has examined it, when each examination occurred and what tests were carried out. This is important as one test may influence the validity of any subsequent observation on the sample.

FORENSIC DATA

THE COLUMBINE HIGH SCHOOL SHOOTING

Some crimes trigger such a huge response that no one lab or team is big enough to cope. In April 1999, two students went on a shooting spree at Columbine High School, Colorado, US, killing 12 other students and a teacher before committing suicide. Officers arrived within minutes of reports of the first shots being fired, and eventually 615 officers from 27 law enforcement agencies converged on the scene. Despite such a large response, officers were unable to secure the school and evacuate all victims until about four and a half hours after attending the scene. As well as being armed, the two students had planted homemade bombs all around the building which made it necessary for the authorities to enter each room in the school, over 250 of them, one by one. The forensic team moved in and a task force of over 100 detectives from a dozen local, state and federal law enforcement agencies conducted 4,500 interviews with students, teachers, parents and others. Other experts used computers to enhance grainy videotape footage to establish exactly how and why the tragedy had occurred.

THE CRIME SCENE

Forensic science begins at the crime scene. But sometimes
the extent of that scene can be difficult to pin down, and
the evidence hard to find. Even in relatively straightforward
cases, the forensic investigator's motto must be:
Think out of the box.

There may be a body on the floor of a flat, a weapon 3 feet (1 metre)
away, and an apparent assailant sitting stupefied in a corner of the same
room. This is a scene of a crime, but not a crime scene. The crime scene
can easily be much more. Yes, it may be confined to that one room, but it
could include the whole flat or even the entire building. It may also cover
the route through the city used by the murderer to reach the room, or the
interior of the taxi hired by the victim to transport illicit drugs earlier in
the day.

Some crime scenes are far bigger than this. In the case of a plane
crash, the place where the plane fell to earth is obviously important, but
so is the path followed by the plane in the minutes before it tumbled
from the air. The ground below, scattered with pieces of evidence that
will help experts make sense of the incident, is just as much a part of the
crime scene as the plane's final resting place. Likewise, the site of a road
traffic accident may be in the middle of a busy way, but the crime scene
may include the half-mile of road along which the vehicles involved in
the crash skidded before coming to a halt.

Alternatively, the scene of the crime may be tiny, perhaps restricted
to a phone booth that can be taken away in its entirety for examination,
or a computer laptop, which can be slipped into a plastic bag. Whatever

It is the first responder's task to alert the emergency services to the incident, to deal with dead or injured people at the scene, and to initiate crime-scene security.

the extent of the scene, however, there are some basic principles that must be followed from the moment the police arrive.

THE FIRST RESPONDER

Crimes, accidents, disasters and other incidents that require police and forensic assistance can take many forms. The first responder – most often a local police officer, though it could be a member of the public – has to think fast to apply general principles to the specific situation:

Save lives and ensure safety

The first responder needs to look around and take in details quickly. How many victims are there? Are the victims dead, dazed, injured or behaving

At a crime scene a perimeter is usually established with tape or rope to restrict access and prevent evidence being lost or destroyed.

aggressively? Is the assailant still at the crime scene? The first responder's priority now is to act quickly to save lives and ensure safety for everyone present, while at the same time touching as little as possible, to preserve precious evidence. These aims may be complicated if a crime is still in progress or a criminal remains near the scene. In either case, the first responder needs to be aware that there is every chance the criminal may be desperate and strike again in order to escape. Are there people who witnessed the event who need to be interviewed either at the scene or at a later date? The first responder should also be prepared to take field notes as his or her first impressions of the scene may be crucial to the outcome.

Make the area safe

The first responder needs to assess the situation according to the scene found. For example, if the scene involves a vehicle, then the first person to arrive turns off the ignition and checks for any petrol leaks that could trigger a fire. If there has been an explosion in a building, then special attention needs to be given to checking for a gas leak or exposed wiring that could harm someone or trigger a fire. The first responder warns people if there is a risk of injury from escaped chemicals or gases, and tries to keep people well away from the area until backup arrives. These safety checks become particularly important if terrorists are thought to be involved. If an explosion has occurred, there may be a second device hidden in the locality and timed to go off just as the rescue effort is starting. It is also possible that the area has been booby-trapped, so checking for suspicious wires and packages is a priority.

Preserve the evidence

The first responder's actions aim to leave evidence untampered with. Any victims are given first aid, but they must avoid washing or removing clothing because doing so could remove splashes of blood, strands of hair or fragments of skin that have come from the attacker. These are valuable pieces of evidence, and specialist forensic officers will collect and preserve them as soon as possible. The first responder must also ensure that the testimonial evidence of witnesses to the crime is recorded in detail.

Record details

Backup will probably come from paramedic teams, and the first responder keeps a record of hospitals where anyone hurt in the incident has been taken, possibly sending a police officer with the ambulances so that victims don't get "lost" from follow-up.

FORENSIC DATA

THE OJ SIMPSON TRIAL

The case of OJ Simpson highlights that if forensic evidence is to be admissable in a court of law, the highest professional standards must be observed at the scene of the crime.

The 1995 trial of OJ Simpson found flaws in the way the initial response police procedures were handled. Simpson had been accused of murdering his former wife, Nicole Brown Simpson, on June 12, 1994. At Simpson's home police found evidence of blood and entered without a permit, an action permissible because the situation was an emergency. Where the police went wrong was to collect a pair of blood-stained gloves during that visit. Collecting evidence without proper permits became one of the arguments used by Simpson's defence team that led to his acquittal.

Detain suspects

Once victims are protected and cared for, there's a chance of detaining a suspect. Not every criminal flees from a scene as soon as a crime is committed. Many hang around, perhaps to cover their tracks and confuse evidence, or to commit further violence.

Release the scene

Once authorities arrive it's time for the first responder to hand over, but the job is not completely finished. The first responder is the first person that the crime team interviews, and is in the best position to rapidly give them the information they need to take over smoothly. The officer makes sure his or her notes are clear while the events are still very recent, and checks any sketch maps he or she has made. Among the first responder's notes are weather conditions, including any changes in the weather that may have occurred before the investigative team arrived.

Suspects and witnesses

More backup arrives. Investigating officers search any suspects detained in the locality, and all items of interest, including clothing, is seized for later analysis. Depending on the nature of the crime, this task may be done by specialist forensic experts or a local police officer. Whoever does it, the principles remain the same. Everything is carefully bagged and documented so that investigators can use an object in a subsequent trial. Documents should include notes about the object's condition when found, and where or from whom it came. Poor documentation effectively means no evidence, because an accused person's defence team will be able to cast doubt on when and where it was collected.

Protecting the crime scene means keeping as many people away as possible – especially anyone who may be linked with the incident.

SECURING A CRIME SCENE

Securing the physical scene is an important part of the first responder's role. As much as possible he or she should keep an eye on any exits and entrances, and note people and vehicles that have been coming and going, along with a record of the times. This information will be invaluable to the investigating team. The first responder now needs to secure the scene to avoid the deliberate or unintentional interference with physical items.

1. If the scene is out of doors, the first responder may lay a cloth or waterproof sheet carefully over evidence if it looks liable to damage.

2. Press and non-involved police officers are kept out, because the more people who enter the area, the greater the likelihood of contaminating the scene and destroying evidence. Also, if media reports contain too much detail of the incident, they could jeopardise any future trial. It may be that the crime scene is so open to view that police need to erect barriers such as tents to block off sight lines.

3. There is probably a fairly well-defined primary site, but there may also be secondary sites. The first responder must identify a route in and out of these zones to avoid the crime sites, and as other support personnel arrive, show them where to walk. This minimises the chance of ruining evidence. Records are kept of everyone who arrives at, or leaves, the site.

4. Any unusual smells or strange sounds are noted. If the crime scene is in a room, it may be that someone recently there had a powerful body odour

Police secure the scene of a fatal shooting to prevent vital evidence being lost or damaged. Investigating officers also mark areas of special interest to the case, either with cones, chalk or other markers.

or was wearing a particular fragrance. The smell could easily have vanished by the time the rest of the team arrive, so the first responder may be the only one who has a chance of picking it up.

5. The first responder makes sure that the area is enclosed, ensuring all entrances and exits are covered. Colleagues start to take some of the load now, but these new arrivals can also contaminate the area. Visitors to the site must wear protective overalls to avoid cross-contamination.

Suspects are, as far as possible, prevented from returning to the scene of the crime. If they were not, suspects could later claim, for example, that footprints and other apparent evidence connecting them with the incident were left during the rescue attempts made immediately after the event.

Police ensure that eyewitness statements are independent of one another by keeping bystanders away from suspects, and if necessary encouraging bystanders not to talk to others, particularly other witnesses, about what they think happened. Witnesses talking among themselves could influence one another's memories, which would mean that nothing they say can be used in the courts. The investigator's job here is to ensure that if a suspect is caught and tried, defence lawyers will have little opportunity to cast doubt on eyewitness evidence. Not everyone will be

FORENSIC DATA

LEGAL CONSIDERATIONS: THE CASE OF RUFUS MINCEY

There is little point in collecting evidence if a judge throws out the information it reveals because the investigators broke the law when they collected it. In 1978, a court in Arizona reviewed the conviction of Rufus Mincey. He'd been convicted of killing an undercover policeman who had broken into his apartment while trying to bust a drug gang. Police spent four days at the apartment gathering various items including drugs and bullets, but did this without a search warrant. At the appeal hearing the court acquitted Mincey because under the Fourth Amendment police are required to have a warrant, and this requirement cannot be waived just because the crime is considered serious.

willing to act as a witness, either because they don't want to relive the trauma of the event, or they're afraid of reprisals. They may be reluctant to come forward at a later date if investigators make a plea for information. Recording names and addresses of people while they are still at the scene can give follow-up teams a much greater chance of finding them when other investigators need to get in touch.

COMBING THE AREA

With the scene secure and marked off with tape, ropes and flags, it's time to search for evidence. A detailed sketch map is a good starting place. An officer measures the distance of items of furniture from walls.

The search

The investigative team must get the search right first time, because there often isn't a second chance. Searchers disturb an area as they go over it, so the only time they can get a true impression of what the place was like when the crime occurred is the initial search. Thoroughness is combined with speed. A public street or road can't remain closed forever, and needs to be released as soon as possible. In addition, some types of evidence – skid marks on a road, for example – may degrade quickly. Officers must decide what constitutes useful evidence. They cannot simply package up everything they find, so this filtering process is important. There is no point overwhelming the forensic laboratory with hundreds of items – as overloading them could mean that key finds are overlooked.

The nature of the crime influences decisions about how to start searching. A murder indoors may require only a local search of the room, but a bomb explosion in a shopping mall may scatter evidence far and wide. However, there are general rules.

Search methods

1. Officers start by searching any outdoor area so that evidence can't be destroyed by the weather. In addition, public places have priority because they are more difficult to secure and need to be handed over more quickly. Searches of entry and exit routes often yield more evidence than peripheral areas. If a search is needed around a body before it can be removed, then that is of high priority.

2. For wide-open spaces such as parks and fields, investigators can adopt the following search methods *(see figs. 1–4, page opp.)* :

👁 **Linear search:**
Investigators walk or crawl slowly forward keeping in a straight line.

👁 **Grid search:**
Two linear sweeps are made over an area, with the second being at right angles to the first.

👁 **Quadrant search:**
The search area is divided up and an investigator is responsible for checking each segment.

👁 **Spiral search:**
Investigators start at the centre of a crime scene and work systematically outward in a spiral formation.

3. Samples of soil can be vital to an investigation. The physical and chemical makeup of soil varies considerably from place to place.

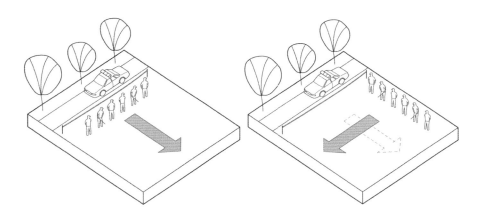

fig. 1 Linear search

fig. 2 Grid search

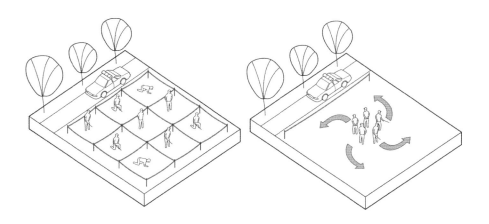

fig. 3 Quadrant search

fig. 4 Spiral search

Experts can match a soil stain on a carpet with samples taken from a suspect's garden, linking that person to the scene. Or, a soil sample from the victim's driveway could show that a suspect's car had been there if experts find similar soil on his car. Soil also contains seeds and pollen, giving clues about the time of year that the clod of earth was lifted from the ground and so narrow down the dates when a suspect was present.

4. It is the job of the investigation team to ensure that items of evidence taken from the scene of a crime are not contaminated or tampered with in any way. For this reason, pieces of evidence need to be kept in special collection bags that reveal if anyone has ever tried to open them to tamper with the evidence. Each collection bag is accompanied by a "chain of custody" document, listing which personnel handled the item at what time, and for what purpose. Without complete documentation of this type, an item of evidence will be regarded as useless in court.

Snap happy

Photography plays a crucial role throughout the search phase. Forensic photographers shoot wide-angle photos of the whole scene to record general layout, and take closeups to record exactly where individual items were discovered, the angle at which they lay, and any features of interest. They will take both black and white and various types of colour print film, and may use both digital and and print cameras. They may also light the scene with special flashes or other types of artificial lighting to ensure they capture as much detail as possible.

Video footage can also be useful in capturing some of the atmosphere of the location, and may help juries to get a feel of what the place was like at the time of the crime. Court cases may occur months or years later, by which time the crime scene could have changed completely.

Photographs should be taken as soon as possible before anything is moved, handled or initiated into the scene. Photographs allow a permanent visual record of the crime scene and items of evidence collected there.

Investigators sift through soil to find evidence left behind by the assailant. Soil samples are often taken from areas surrounding a crime scene for comparison purposes.

In some investigations, still and video images provide the basis for experts to build a model of the scene, or a computer simulation of the event.

Bring in the dogs

Very often the smallest piece of evidence can give the most powerful clue, and you don't get smaller than a few molecules of scent left by a fleeing criminal. No human would ever detect it, but it's easy for a well-trained tracker dog. Police investigators may also use other dogs that have been trained to pick up specific scents – chemicals used to build bombs, for example, or particles of dust that show where illegal drugs have been stored. Dogs can also be skilled in searching out human bodies or their remains by tracking and following the scent of decomposing flesh, or by sniffing for the alcohol present in particular fragrances or the aluminium compounds in some deodorants. The dogs must be introduced to the fragrance or compound before the search begins, so the investigator often requires a sample of clothing from the missing person.

A bloodhound is perhaps the breed of dog that first comes to mind when thinking about tracker dogs, but there is no one breed that works best for each job and condition. A crossbreed might be as skilled at detecting evidence as a pureblood. What all tracker dogs have in common is the ability to find a scent and follow it. The dog is not a pet but a partner to their handler. It is a work associate, and the specialised handler must be as skilled at translating and communicating the evidence as the dog is at discovering it.

Special locations

Some scene-of-crime locations require specialist search teams. Police divers may be brought in to search for a firearm dumped in a river. Divers must be ready to work in and adapt to the conditions at hand, including the temperature of the water, varying levels of visibility and potentially dangerous wreckage or obstacles in the water. They may also be called on to recover human bodies.

Investigators equipped with metal detectors may locate jewellery left on a buried victim, or helicopter-mounted thermal-imaging cameras which can be used from a distance and see through all kinds of barriers, including water, darkness and solid objects, could spot the heat coming from a hidden suspect or a decomposing body. Air-crash investigators are often required to collect thousands of fragments of wreckage and piece them together to form a reconstruction of the original aircraft.

RECONSTRUCTIONS

Revisiting a crime scene and replaying the events can help the investigation in several ways. It may shed light on how many people were involved in the event, how long different activities associated with the crime probably took, and exactly who stood where in the sequence of events. And just getting a person to walk along the route taken by a victim can jog witnesses' memories.

A reconstruction can determine whether witness statements are accurate. For example, police can find out whether people really could see particular actions given the locations they claimed to be in at the time. If the reconstruction shows that a statement is implausible, the investigators must decide whether the witness is lying, or is imagining what they think happened, rather than simply recounting what actually happened.

A good reconstruction can only take place if physical evidence at the scene has already been carefully itemised and catalogued, and analysed alongside statements from witnesses and those involved in the incident. Without this, replaying the event is just down to guesswork, and will have limited power. Where possible, the reconstruction is staged at the same time of day as the initial event, and under similar weather conditions. If the event involved a person walking down an alley after dark, it's best to stage the reconstruction at night because, for example, the lack of light might affect the amount of time it takes to walk from one end of the alley to the other. Witnesses (or actors) take up their original positions and play out

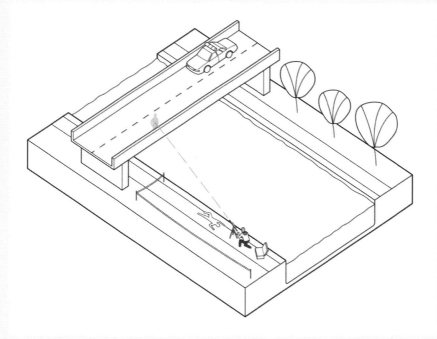

A laser beam is used to simulate the proposed trajectory of a bullet showing the likely position that the assailant stood on the bridge overhead.

their actions to the best of their memory. A reconstruction may also help police find more evidence. Police may use a mannequin with a hole carefully drilled to match the path taken by a bullet in the victim's body. Placing it where the victim appears to have been when shot allows investigators to shine a laser beam back through the hole and pinpoint where the assailant was most probably positioned when the trigger was pulled. Pointing the laser in the other direction may lead investigators to the bullet's final resting place.

Blood spatter patterns can also be important as the way that blood lands depends on the nature and sequence of different injuries.

PHYSICAL EVIDENCE

Physical evidence includes anything that can establish that a crime has been committed or provide a link between crime and suspect, or crime and victim. It could be as massive as an 18-ton truck or as tiny as a grain of pollen. A good evidence collector will not approach a scene with a predetermined expectation of what can be found.

There are two ways that physical evidence is useful: to identify the nature of specific items or to compare two or more samples to see if they match.

IDENTIFICATION

Criminalists get a huge amount of information from a tiny sample. Given a fragment of plastic, they can look at the physical and chemical characteristics of the item and suggest what object it may have come from. This can be useful in a positive and negative sense. For example, finding that gunshot residue comes from a type of cartridge frequently used by a particular suspect for sports target practice could be important, but it would be of great interest to the defence team to discover that the residue came from a make of ammunition not used by the suspect. Other substances commonly tested are:

Drugs
Testing the composition of a white powder may show that it's an illicit or prescription drug. Scientists need to determine what type of drug it is – heroin, cocaine or barbiturates – or a commonly used painkiller.

Fibres

In the case of suspected arson, fragments of cloth found where the fire officers believe the fire may have started could have petrol residues lingering in the fabric.

Explosives and residues

Burn marks at the site of an explosion may reveal particles of specific explosives or the chemicals they normally leave behind. The examination of gunshot residues on hands and around gunshot wounds can point to a particular gun or incriminate a suspect.

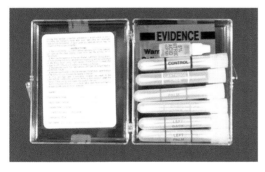

An atomic absorption analysis kit is used to detect firearm discharge residue on skin or clothing.

Hair

Samples of hair may be important. Looking down a microscope at pieces of hair is often all it takes to show whether a sample has come from a human or an animal. If it is found to be human, the hair may be subjected to more technical investigations using DNA analysis to give a more detailed understanding of who it came from.

Ideally, these kinds of assessments should be a matter of pure scientific evidence with no judgment needed. In reality, life is seldom that simple, and samples arriving in a forensics laboratory are often contaminated with dirt, or have degraded in some way. As a result, final decisions about samples require a fair amount of art and experience in addition to scientific techniques.

COMPARISON

Experts are also called upon to compare physical evidence, either with libraries of known samples held in the lab, or with other evidence connected with the crime. The question here is whether two or more of the samples came from the same place. This can be resolved by seeing if a sample recovered from a crime scene matches samples collected from a suspect or victim. Again, a match could confirm that a suspect was at the scene, but finding that the hair couldn't have come from the suspect tells you that either he wasn't there or was accompanied by someone else.

Comparing physical evidence is a two-stage process. In the first, the forensic scientist performs a range of tests on the samples. In the second, investigators form an opinion of whether the results indicate that the two samples have a common origin.

Individual characteristics

Making these comparisons often comes down to a question of probability – what's the likelihood of the apparent match happening by chance? Juries may be faced with an expert witness testifying that there is a one-in-a-million probability that a particular match occurred by chance. The information can appear compelling, but defence lawyers will remind jurors that the chance of winning a national lottery is often set at odds of around one in 14 million. The fact that in most weeks someone does win shows that even highly improbable coincidences can occur.

The forensic scientist's task is to find a set of tests that show that the chance of a random match is unlikely. This means looking for aspects of a sample that vary widely within a population, but are fixed within a single person or object. Where a characteristic can point to a definite link with next to no doubt, it's called an "individual characteristic".

What are "individual characteristics"?

🖐 Fingerprints: This is one of the classic examples of individual characteristics, as there is virtually no chance of two people ever having identical prints – not even identical twins. Comparing a fingerprint collected at a scene with one taken from a suspect in a police station is a powerful way of using physical evidence.

🖐 Bullet striations: Matching the scratches on a bullet with imperfections in the barrel of a gun is a convincing way of linking a firearms offence to an individual weapon.

🖐 Footprints: Crimes have been solved by looking at the fine detail of the tread on a person's shoes and matching it to footprints found next to a victim.

🖐 Other significant marks: Scratches on the side of the broken tip of a penknife blade can be shown to line up with scratches on a broken penknife found in a suspect's trouser pocket. In one case, lines running through the black plastic bin-liner that had been wrapped around a victim proved that the bag had been part of a roll found in a suspect's kitchen.

Class characteristics

All too often, this tight link between the two samples of evidence proves elusive, so forensic investigators need to look further. Information can be gained by looking at the "class" of an item. An empty cigarette packet found near the victim, for example, could belong to the same brand and type that a suspect is known to smoke. On its own, this piece of physical evidence doesn't link the suspect to the crime, but it's one clue that can be added to any assessment of the probability that this particular person was involved in the crime.

Data from class characteristics has the advantage of being free from personal bias – it simply exists – and interpretation becomes a matter of assessment; the decision ultimately rests with a jury. The problem here is that once again, faced by a seemingly infallible forensic scientist, juries

CLASS EVIDENCE IN PRACTICE

You leave your car in a supermarket car park. When you return there is a scrape all the way down one side. You want to know who did it, so that you can pursue them for the cost of repair.

1. The red paint scrape on your white car is a piece of class physical evidence, ruling out every car that's not coloured red. If the crime were important enough, a laboratory would analyse the chemical makeup of the paint to reveal the manufacturer, the model of the car, and perhaps even the vehicle's age.

2. The scrape is high on the side of your car, suggesting a large, off-road-type vehicle, and definitely ruling out low-slung sports cars – another piece of class evidence.

3. A piece of broken glass from an indicator bulb is not from your car as your lights are intact. Moulded into the plastic is the name, Ford. Class evidence again, but the class is narrowing.

4. Now you are on the track of a large red Ford with a broken indicator light. You may even get lucky and find it parked somewhere else in the car park.

may give too much weight to an individual piece of evidence. There is, after all, a world of difference between saying that a piece of physical evidence indicates a possibility that the suspect and a particular item of evidence are linked, and saying that the two are definitely tied together. However, class evidence can form a web of connections that eventually catches the fly.

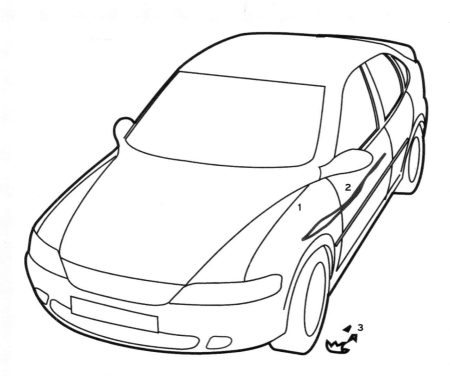

Collating items of class physical evidence can help to build up a picture of a suspect. In this case the paint colour, position and make of the suspect car provides vital leads.

Individual or class?

The problem with class evidence is its imprecision since it does not identify any one person. Individual evidence does that. Sometimes improvements to methods of analysis give more accurate information about an item of evidence, so that the item moves category. For example, blood samples used to be divided into classes according to blood groups (A, B, O, AB). This division was useful, but as millions of people share the same blood groups it was imprecise. With the advent of genetic technology, experts can now look at the DNA makeup of cells within each sample. This type of evidence points with much greater precision to an individual person. Blood smears can now be individual, rather than class, physical evidence.

The point at which an item of physical evidence crosses the boundary from being a piece of class evidence to a piece of individual evidence is difficult to assess and is often argued between forensic scientists and police investigators. A positive outcome to an investigation will come down to a question of extensive background research to determine the likelihood of two items matching, even though they come from different sources.

The issue is not only how many identical items there are, but also the chance of that item being found in a particular location. Looking at the packet of cigarettes again, a tobacco manufacturer makes millions of packets of a brand of cigarettes every year. Just finding a packet could indicate that one of thousands of people could have dropped it. If, however, the packet was of an unusual brand of Brazilian cigarettes and was discovered at the scene of a crime in Scotland then the finger of suspicion would point more strongly at a businessman or woman who, perhaps, made frequent journeys to South America and was known to smoke cigarettes.

COMMON PHYSICAL TRACES AND THEIR SIGNIFICANCE

- **Blood, semen and saliva:** all contain DNA

- **Hair:** can be matched microscopically

- **Body organ samples:** may reveal traces of poisons

- **Fingerprints:** a classic identifier

- **Documents:** letters and e-mails link people

- **Serial numbers:** can indicate if item has been stolen

- **Impressions:** from crowbar marks, knife cuts, footprints, tire tracks

- **Glass:** fragments are easy to compare

- **Soil and minerals:** can be highly specific to an area

- **Fibres:** can link suspect and crime scene

- **Petroleum residues:** indication of arson

- **Paint, plastic and rubber:** all have unique chemical compositions

- **Powder residues:** from firearm discharge or drugs

- **Firearms and explosives:** possession strongly implicates individuals in a crime

- **Wood and other vegetative fragments:** presence on clothing, shoes and tools can link suspect and crime scene

PRESERVED FOR THE COURT

If an item of physical evidence is worth collecting, then it is important, where possible, to pick up a large enough sample for a battery of tests to be carried on it. There are two main reasons for this:

🗁 Tests on large samples are cheaper to carry out than tests on small ones.

🗁 The defence team may well ask for part of the sample so that they can perform their own tests.

Retrieving samples

When gathering samples of evidence there are some basic errors to avoid. If, for example, a door jamb has clear marks showing where someone used a crowbar to wrench it open, and a crowbar is found lying nearby, it would seem natural for police on the scene to try to fit the two together to see if they match. But doing so would be a terrible mistake since this would contaminate both the door jamb and the crowbar, effectively destroying both pieces of evidence. The door jamb should be carefully removed and, along with the crowbar, both pieces of evidence should be taken away for laboratory scientists to examine.

Storing samples

Evidence samples must be treated correctly. They must be stored separately from one another in controlled conditions, keeping them away from sources of light and high temperatures. Some samples of evidence will require special storage conditions, including refrigeration, to be handled only by a forensics expert.

To avoid the possibility of cross-contamination investigators use sterile gloves to bag up evidence at a crime scene. Forensic evidence bags have protective tamperproof seals.

USING SOIL COMPARISON TECHNIQUES

California is a state known for its beaches, and if you live near the coast it's a fair bet that at least a few grains of sand will be imbedded in your carpets. In such a location, a forensic search team that spots a small pile of sand on the carpet could be forgiven for ignoring it. But the sand may still be worth collecting, because there's a possibility that analysis will show that it comes not from the locality, but from some other part of the state or even interstate. If there's already evidence that the perpetrator came from this same distant location, then this additional information could prove his or her downfall.

Assessing a soil sample starts with a simple visual inspection comparing its colour and texture with other samples. After that it can be checked out using a light microscope, which can show up seeds and tiny animals, such as mites, that may give clues about its origins. If there are questions about the date when a crime occurred, these biological elements of the soil can be very useful, as many are only present at certain times of the year.

High-powered electron microscopes provide 3-D pictures of very small items such as pollen, and identify the underlying rock type in the area a sample came from. Alternatively, running a sample through a series of sieves can divide it into its constituent parts, producing another way of

A person at a crime scene will inevitably pick up trace evidence from the location on his clothing. Hairs, fibres, dust, soil, sand or plant debris have all been used to trap criminals.

comparing two batches. It's very unlikely that two samples of soil will divide up into the same set of components by chance. If there's a match, there's most probably a reason. More technical methods, such as X-ray diffraction or chemical analysis, provide more information.

A rape case in Canada was solved when lab scientists found significant differences in the soil samples taken from the two knees of a suspect's pair of jeans. At first, they didn't know how this could have occurred, but when they compared these contrasting soils with material collected from two knee impressions found at the crime scene they found that the soil in the left and right impressions matched the respective stains in the jeans. For this match to occur by chance was very unlikely – the suspect, or at least his jeans, had to have been at the crime scene.

SCIENTIFIC ANALYSIS OF SAMPLES

Over the last century, science has made huge inroads into forensic investigations. Any method of categorising or analysing material that has been developed for general science has found its way into a forensic laboratory. Science has the following three basic concepts that underlie it.

Empirical evidence

Scientists say that their work is empirical, meaning that its findings and theories are based only and entirely on observations and recorded experience. To claim that you know something, you need to see it – to in some way experience a physical event. You can have theories about how something must work, or what events occurred, but for your argument to have any strength, to be able to convict the person responsible for the crime in question, the theories need to be supported by solid evidence.

Test conditions

Science brings with it the assumption that there is a rational world that operates according to a standard set of rules and principles. This means that a scientist can perform a test on a substance and be sure that under the same conditions the substance will always react in the way observed in the test. For example, an iron bar placed in water takes a certain time to rust to pieces, so a similar object placed in that sort of water will fall apart at the same rate. There are many scientists who specialise in studying the specific and universal features of the way items behave in different situations. If, for example, you take a decaying body to the correct specialist, and tell him or her some details about the place it was found and the weather conditions over the previous days, weeks and months, the expert will be able to draw a reasonably accurate conclusion about how long the body has lain there.

Standardisation

If a scientific assessment has been done well, then it shouldn't make any difference who performed the test. Anyone skilled in operating a particular piece of scientific equipment, and who follows agreed methods, should get the same results when they analyse a sample. The admissibility of forensic evidence in cases is based on this understanding. Both the prosecution and defence teams should get the same findings when they test any piece of evidence.

WHAT AND HOW MUCH?

A large part of the work of a forensic laboratory is identifying the material that makes up a piece of evidence. This could be because investigators need to know exactly what it is, or because they want to use this information to compare two or more samples. Scientists have a massive array of tests that can help.

Scientific techniques are good at asking two different questions. What sort of materials are present in a sample? And how much of each type of material is present? In analysing a drug sample, for example, the first analysis could tell you that there is some ecstasy and some talcum powder, the second would tell you the proportion of each. Both assessments have their uses in different situations. Such examinations won't always solve cases but may confirm or strengthen them.

CHROMATOGRAPHY

To work out what a material is, or to compare it with other similar objects, scientists often use techniques that break up the material into its individual elements, and then look at the ingredients. Chromatography is one of many different tools that perform this task. It's used to identify chemicals as different as dyes, drugs and residues found in dirt. This method can also identify genes, proteins and DNA from tiny samples which can aid investigators as they track down criminals. A lab will have a number of different chromatography machines, but they are all based on a similar scientific principle.

Gas chromatography and high-performance liquid chromatography (HPLC)

Using these methods the scientist places a sample in a vaporiser, and a stream of inert gas then blows the vaporised particles through a tube. The tube design varies. It will either be packed with granular particles of material like sand, and about ⅛ inch (3 millimetres) wide and 6 to 20 feet (2 to 6 metres) long, or empty but only about 0.5 millimetre in diameter and up to 200 feet (60 metres) long. In both cases, the interior of the tube is coated with a fine layer of a liquid.

When you vaporise a material, you heat it up so that it will turn from a solid into a gas. This allows all the different components of the sample to move on their own. Each of these different components behaves very differently inside the tube, and these differences can be used to separate them out. Some components will prefer to stay in the gas and avoid binding with the liquid. They will race quickly through the tube. Others will bind to the liquid and be a bit reluctant to go with the flow of gas. These will take longer to pass along the tube.

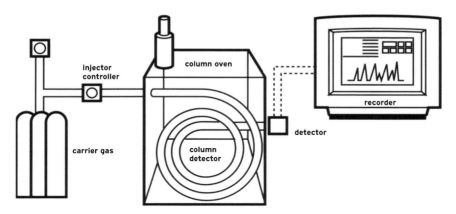

Gas chromatography separates substances according to their movement when carried by gas through a thin film of liquid.

Using a detector at the end of the tube, scientists measure how long it takes for each component to pass through the tube. When they compare this with times taken for known substances, they can get a good idea of what was in the sample. Part of the power of this technique is that only tiny amounts of a sample are needed to get a good reading. This accuracy, however, can be its downfall. Anything in the sample will give a reading, so dirt or dust can easily contaminate a piece of evidence if it's not handled carefully.

Thin-layer chromatography

Another way of making use of the way that molecules behave when they are dissolved is to use thin-layer chromatography. A scientist places a dot of the sample at one end of a sheet of plastic or glass that has a thin layer of a granular material spread on it. The scientist then stands the sheet upright in liquid, which is placed in a closed chamber. As the liquid seeps up the thin layer it dissolves the sample and carries it up the sheet. The different components in the sample travel at different rates and soon

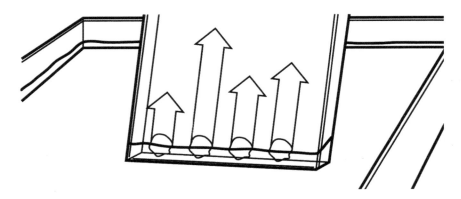

Thin-layer chromatography separates substances by the speed at which they move by capillary action up a plate covered with silica gel.

separate. You can see the same effect by putting a dot of water-soluble ink from a felt pen onto paper and then standing it in water. As the water rises it separates the ink into the different pigments that make up the colour. If you try this with two red inks from different manufacturers you will find that they separate into two distinct sets of pigments.

ELECTROPHORESIS

Another way of separating components within a sample is electrophoresis. This technique is particularly good at separating proteins. It does this based on the size and shape of each protein.

Biological samples are dotted onto a book-sized glass plate coated in a layer of gel-like material. An electric current is passed though the plate, and this current tugs molecules across it, the friction force of the gel acting as a kind of sieve, separating the molecules by size. All proteins carry an electrical charge and those with a large charge will travel fastest. Also, small proteins travel faster than large ones.

Once the proteins have been separated, a small section of the gel can be cut out and sent off for further analysis. This method is particularly good for isolating biological molecules. Blood or semen samples may be run through this test as the number and position of bands formed on each lane of gel is the actual genetic "fingerprint" of that DNA sample.

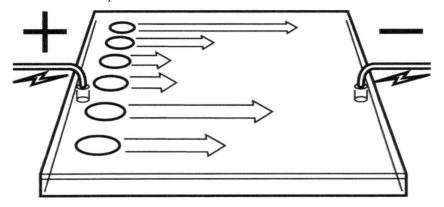

Gel electrophoresis is a method that separates protein molecules on the basis of their size, electrical charge and other physical properties.

SPECTROPHOTOMETRY

One of the main aims of forensic science is to identify the chemical composition of substances with a high degree of certainty. The techniques so far described separate the different constituents of a sample. To find out what exactly these constituents are, forensic scientists use a spectrophotometer. This machine makes use of the properties of light. Shining a beam of light through a prism splits the light into a rainbow of colours – red, orange, yellow, green, blue, indigo, violet. These are all present in the original beam, but when seen together, simply look white.

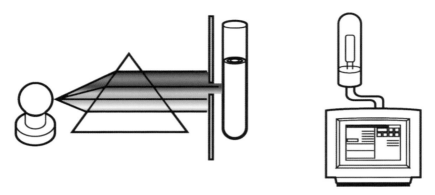

Spectrophotometers consist of a light source beamed through a prism and a sample which is decoded electrically and the output recorded in the form of a line graph.

When you look at an object it appears to have a colour because the material it's made of absorbs all the other colours in the light, and reflects the ones that you see. If something looks red, this is because it absorbs most of the violet, blues, greens and yellows, and just reflects red. Criminalists can use this absorption and reflection of light to glean valuable information about the nature of a sample.

Using a spectrophotometer, experts can see exactly which colours of light are affected by a sample, and then compare this information with samples of material that they already know about. One advantage of using a machine over using our eyes is that a spectrophotometer can detect the effect that objects have on infrared and ultraviolet light, neither of which can be seen by our eyes. This means it can make a much more thorough assessment than we could ever do just by looking at the sample. This technique is often used to analyse drugs. If faced with a white powder, a scientist first runs spectrophotometer tests on it, then compares the light the powder absorbs with the known value of light absorbed by, say, cocaine. If the two values are similar, the powder is probably cocaine.

Other related techniques involve heating the sample so that, in effect, it starts to glow. A scientist can then assess the light that's given off. The colour of light emitted is specific for specific elements, so this emission spectrometry gives valuable information about the elements present in the material.

MASS SPECTROMETRY

A mass spectrometer is a machine that draws the sample into a chamber, and then bombards the molecules with high-energy electrons that, like two pool balls striking each other, knock electrons out of the sample molecules. The loss of these electrons makes the molecules become unstable and they fall to pieces. The mass spectrometer then uses a magnetic or electrical field to measure the mass of each piece.

A particular molecule will always break into the same range of pieces, and there is next to no chance that two different molecules will break into the same sets. Therefore, the result is that an experienced forensic specialist should be able to take a sample of material and tell exactly what chemical it is.

NEUTRON ACTIVATION ANALYSIS

Neutron activation analysis is one of the most sensitive tests in the scientist's analytical armoury. This technique looks at the heart of the atoms in a sample, exposing it to gamma rays, before determining what atoms are present. It can tell whether atoms of particular elements are present right down to levels as low as one part per billion. Forensic scientists use it to detect trace elements in metals, drugs, paint, soil, gunpowder and hair.

FORENSIC DATA

THE HITLER DIARIES

In the early 1980s, a German publisher paid $2.3 million for 60 handwritten notebooks that comprised the diaries of Adolf Hitler. These works were astonishing, as they indicated that Hitler had been oblivious to "the final solution", the Nazi extermination of Europe's Jews; in fact, he had wanted to resettle the Jews in the East. History needed rewriting.

The origin of the documents was a mystery. Apparently they had left Berlin toward the end of World War II, but the plane had crashed. Some farmers found the documents, which eventually came into the possession of Konrad Kujau, a collector of Nazi documents. Kujau then took them to Gerd Heidemann, a journalist on Germany's *Stern* newspaper. On April 22, 1983, *Stern* began serialising their shocking scoop. The company also sold publication rights to *Newsweek* in America and to *The Sunday Times* in London.

The owner of *The Sunday Times*, however, had serious doubts about their authenticity, and called for tests. Handwriting experts compared all the documents with each other, and with other known examples of Hitler's

X-RAY DIFFRACTION

While neutron activation analysis can tell you what elements are present in a sample, they can't tell you anything about the way these are arranged. It is the precise three-dimensional lattice of elements that gives a material its properties. A technique called X-ray diffraction, however, can provide clues about the atomic structure of a substance.

work. The experts concluded that the documents were indeed authentic. (What they didn't realise at the time was that they were comparing the documents with other faked versions of Hitler's writing.)

But laboratory analysis of the chemicals used in the paper and ink told another story. West German police shone ultraviolet light on the paper and found that it contained a substance that had been added to paper only since 1954. Spectrophotometric tests on the ink determined the absorption spectrum of the pigment, and thin-layer chromatography revealed its exact composition. The conclusion was clear. This ink had not been available during the war. In addition, threads in seals on the documents contained chemicals that were only manufactured after the war. Then a test that involved evaporating chloride from the ink indicated that the documents had been written within the past year.

The forger turned out to be Konrad Kujau, who had perfected the art of imitating Hitler's handwriting. Heidemann was also accused of having embezzled some of the money paid for the diaries, and both men were sentenced to over four years in prison.

In this technique, X-rays are fired at a sample. These collide with the sample's atoms and bounce off, hitting a sheet of photographic paper. The way the X-rays bounce is set by the nature of the atoms they strike, but every material will produce a unique pattern on the photograph – a unique diffraction pattern. The technique of X-ray diffraction is powerful so long as there is at least five percent of the material you want to analyse within a sample. At lower levels than this, the technique will not yield any useful information.

THE ASSASSINATION OF JOHN F KENNEDY

Neutron activation analysis was used in the investigation into the assassination of president John F Kennedy in 1963. One question has long hung over this crime. How many people were involved? Lee Harvey Oswald was arrested for the murder, but many suspected that he didn't act alone. One aspect of this speculation is that Kennedy was not the only person hit; a bullet also struck Governor Connally as he travelled in the president's car.

It is generally thought by today's forensic pathologists that the investigation into this case had been handled in an incompetent manner. The autopsy had been superficial and the investigation incomplete. When the old files were investigated, it was discovered that certain key items were missing: photographs of Kennedy's internal chest wounds, glass slides of his skin wound, and most importantly, President Kennedy's brain.

The Warren Commission, set up to investigate the shooting, concluded that Oswald fired three bullets. One missed and was lost. One hit the president in the back before going on to strike the governor. One struck the president in his head. But critics of the commission are sceptical that a single bullet wounded both the president and the governor. Doesn't it make more sense, they ask, to say that the wounds attributed to a single bullet were a result of two bullets fired from different places?

To try to answer these doubts, forensic scientists in 1979 used neutron activation analysis to analyse the metal in the two recovered

Though the two bullets that wounded Kennedy had minor differences in their composition, they were almost certainly fired from the same gun.

bullets and in several metal fragments taken from the two men's wounds. The analysis focused on the metals, silver and antimony, in the bullet pieces that are present in tiny amounts. These trace elements vary considerably from bullet to bullet, but are very similar in pieces of metal from a single slug.

The results showed two distinct clusters of trace elements, with some bullet pieces belonging to one cluster, the rest to the other. This indicated that a single bullet had wounded both men; the other bullet had hit Kennedy only. The experts concluded that there was no reason to disbelieve the Warren Commission's conclusions.

SOURCES OF EVIDENCE

Section 2: page 58

- Hairs, Fibres and Flakes
- Toxicology and Drugs • Serology
- Fingerprints • DNA Analysis • Firearms
- Marks and Impressions • Documents

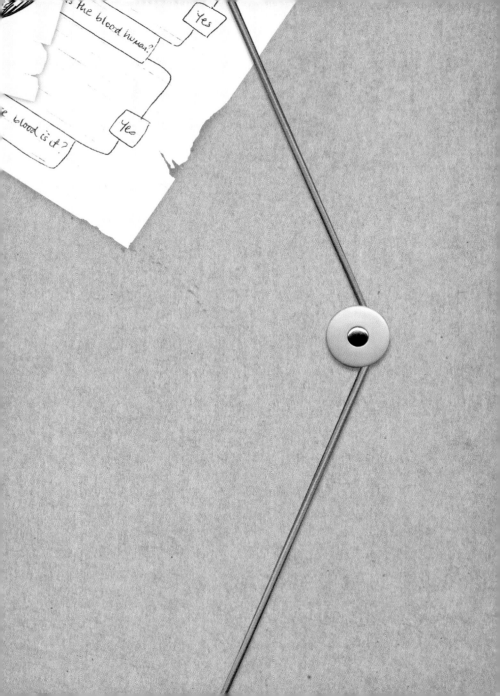

HAIRS, FIBRES AND FLAKES

However much care criminals take, they will invariably leave a trace of their presence at the crime scene. These tiny items can often be the most powerful pieces of evidence. This is certainly the case for strands of hair, particles of synthetic fibres and flecks of paint.

Suction devices are used to collect hair and fibre trace evidence. The investigator wears a glove to prevent contamination of the crime scene.

The more careful a criminal has been, the more observant an investigator has to become. At a crime scene, an investigator may go over the area using a miniature vacuum cleaner fitted with flat filter discs that are regularly replaced and transferred to a sealed, labelled plastic bag. Or investigators may choose to lift hairs, fibres and flakes from a small area by grabbing them on the back of pieces of sticky tape, or if possible, by removing the object they're lying on and taking it back to the controlled conditions of a laboratory where experts can scrape or wash it.

HAIR

It's difficult to stop hair falling from your body. A few strands fall from your head each hour, and if an assailant fights with their victim, there could easily be strands lodged in a fingernail, or bound in with clothing.

How is hair evidence progressed in an investigation?
Retrieval
Strands of hair at a crime scene are picked up with forceps and placed in clip-top bottles. In cases of rape, medical staff use a clean comb to recover any foreign hairs from the victim's pubic region and also take samples of the victim's own hair to act as controls. Investigators may want to pluck up to 50 hairs from each body region of interest from any suspect so that they have a good range of hair for comparison. On occasions, evidence collectors may collect hair from a hairbrush found in a suspect's room.

Comparison
Back at the lab, a criminalist uses a comparison microscope to analyse strands of hair taken from the crime scene with strands from a suspect. The expert places one strand on the microscope stage and another strand

on an adjacent stage. Through the microscope's single viewfinder, both strands can be viewed at high magnification, comparing colour and diameter. By studying the scales that line the exterior of each sample strand, experts can see if the hair strands are similarly arranged.

Although this process allows an expert to judge how similar the two strands are, it can't prove a definite link to an individual person. There's too much variation between hairs within an individual, and too much similarity between people. But hair comparison is still very valuable. To start with, while it may not prove a link between crime-scene samples and a suspect, it can sometimes conclude that the strands found by evidence collectors did not come from a particular individual. This may help police rule out particular people from their enquiries.

Characteristics

Hair analysis may help form an opinion about the assailant's racial background – because hair characteristics vary with race – or may reveal where on the body the hair came from – armpit hair is oval in cross-section, beard hair is triangular, head hair is round, and eyelashes taper rapidly to a point. Looking at the hair root can indicate whether it had been pulled out in a violent struggle, or cut. If there is no root, careful microscopic examination of the cut ends may show what sort of implement had been used. Viewing it with different lights and with spectrophotometry may show if it has been dyed or bleached, which can give a clue about the owner. A strand of hair can also indicate a person's sex, and give a tentative assessment of their age.

Drugs

A strand of hair can also be used as a form of biological diary. If someone takes an illicit drug, for example, a small amount of that drug lodges in

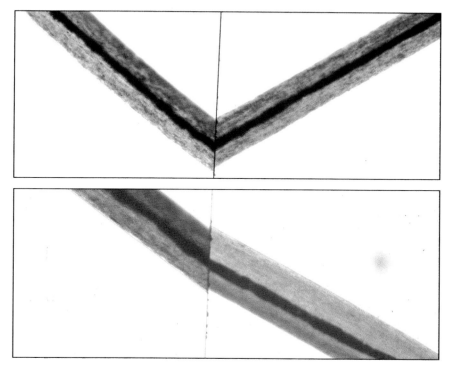

A hair from a suspect and one found on a victim are viewed under a comparison microscope. The image at the bottom shows no match, but the top image shows a positive match.

the millimetre of hair that forms in an average day. In the lab, cutting the hair into small sections, and using mass spectrometry to analyse each section, gives an indication of patterns of drug use, as well as revealing clues about diet and exposure to industrial or environmental chemicals.

Other traces

Finally, hair can also carry other evidence such as traces of dust or blood, fine fibres from fabric, or small particles of paint.

Animal fur

Fur may look similar to human hair, but microscopic examination and careful measurement show that the two are very different. Most fur is finer than human hair, and different species of animals have different characteristic scale patterns on the exterior of the strand. Although finding strands of fur may occasionally help solve a murder or other serious crime, fur is more often significant in cases of animal trafficking, or where law enforcement officers are looking for evidence of misuse of animals in the production of food, clothing or ornaments.

Diatoms (pink) on the fibres (blue) of a burglar's clothing. Diatoms are vital clues to the type of environment the suspect has recently visited.

SYNTHETIC FIBRES

Like hair, natural fibres such as cotton and wool vary greatly within a single sample, and so can't be used to definitely link a crime-scene sample to a suspect. But the machine-made uniformity of synthetic fibres means that analysing synthetics in clothes, seat covers and carpets can give much more conclusive and valuable results. There's a wide range of chemical and physical analyses that can be carried out to characterise a synthetic fibre, and all this information can be used to compare a sample from the crime scene with one taken from a suspect.

How is fibre evidence progressed in an investigation?
Physical makeup
Is it natural or artificial? What is the diameter and shape of each fibre? How many filaments are in a single strand? How big are the filaments? How many times are the filaments twisted over a certain length? What type of dye has been used?

Chemical composition
The chemical composition of a fibre can often be assessed using mass spectrometers, chromatography, or heating the fibre and measuring its melting point. Like hair samples, synthetic fibres may be coated with fragments of other evidence that can be collected and analysed.

Post-crime inspection
Because they are so small and light, fibres can float in the air for hours and even days. This means that investigators often return to a crime scene a few days after the initial inspection to see if any new fibres have settled out. On occasions, crimes have been solved after an investigator has searched through the filters in an office air-conditioning plant and found fibres linked to a suspect who claimed never to have been in a building. Looking for these sorts of lodging places can be particularly useful if the crime occurred a few days or weeks before anyone was aware of it, and the search teams arrive after the area has been disturbed or cleaned.

FORENSIC DATA

THE TRIAL OF IAN HUNTLEY

The 2003 trial in Britain of Ian Huntley, who was accused and found guilty of murdering 10-year-old schoolgirls Holly Wells and Jessica Chapman, turned on fibre evidence. When investigators searched the house he shared with his girlfriend, they found that it had recently been cleaned. The cleaning was so thorough that even though they felt sure the murdered girls had been in the house, they could find no fingerprints.

Although Huntley had gone to great pains to cleanse his house and car, and burn the victims' bodies and clothes, forensic experts still found incriminating fibres. Items in the house or car had 49 fibres matching either Holly's or Jessica's shirt, and 39 fibres matching items found in the car or house were on what remained of Jessica's shirt. They found a further 38 fibres on Holly's shirt and 16 other transfers to or from the girls' tracksuit pants. The dustbin where these pieces of clothing had been found also contained five hairs that matched samples taken from Huntley. The weight of this evidence was such that he was no longer able to claim that he was uninvolved in the crime.

PAINT

A burglar uses a crowbar to force open a window and enter a property. He wears gloves so as not to leave fingerprints, and is careful enough not to leave any other evidence such as footprints, blood, hair or fibres. How do police link this crime with a particular suspect? Paint flecks might provide the answer.

How is paint evidence progressed in an investigation?

Scientists analysing a sample of unknown car paint by comparing it to known paint samples.

Sample match

The police know that tiny flecks of paint from the crowbar-damaged surface of the windowsill probably attached themselves to the burglar's clothing as he climbed through. Criminalists take paint samples from the window and try to link these with flecks of paint from the suspect's clothing. If the two pieces of evidence match, there's a strong probability that they both came from the same place.

Layering

Paint samples can be particularly useful in solving vehicle crimes since the paintwork is often made up of many layers. Police keep databases of compositions and colour ranges used by large vehicle manufacturers. Investigators look at the layering of the flecks under a microscope. Paint is usually applied in three or more layers. A link can be inferred if the examination shows that the samples have identically ordered layers; the possibility of this happening by chance is very small. Also, manufacturers change their formulas frequently, so if a chemical analysis of the paint flecks compares with paints listed in the databases of manufacturers' formulas, a batch of paint can be located in place and time.

In another case, while examining a fleck from a car under a microscope, an expert may notice that the top layer is more loosely bound to the surface than preceding layers, a good indication that the car has had a respray. The police now know to look for a resprayed vehicle.

PAINT ANALYSIS SOLVES ROLEX SHOOTINGS

Flecks of paint from a getaway car led police to two violent robbers who killed one person and wounded three others while stealing two Rolex watches.

In August 2000, Giuseppina Martorana and her husband Giuseppe had been shopping in West London for a pair of rings to celebrate their 25th wedding anniversary. As they returned to their home, two men approached the couple and attempted to steal their Rolex watches. It appears that they had decided to attack the couple while drinking in a nearby restaurant. Giuseppina tried to escape, but was shot in the struggle, and even as she lay dying on the ground one of the attackers pulled the watch from her wrist.

The couple's son Stephen and his girlfriend Isabella were inside the house. They too were shot when they rushed to the front door to see what was going on. The robbers jumped in their car and fled down the street with Giuseppe chasing in his BMW. He didn't stop them, but he did manage to ram the getaway car from the rear.

Soon after the shooting, the police contacted the UK's Major Crime Service and a specialist adviser coordinated all the forensic input. Investigators decided that their best approach would be to try to find the getaway car, and were pleased to find paint left on Giuseppe's damaged car. The paint fleck was unusual as it contained both silver and gold metallic particles. Checks against stolen vehicle reports found that the paint matched a light blue metallic Renault Laguna that had been stolen from a car hire company. On top of this, glass found stuck in the Laguna's fender was similar to the glass in the BMW's broken headlight.

A few months later, a woman handed police a bag of her ex-boyfriend's clothes. These had traces of firearms residue that matched material found on Giuseppina's body and fibres from the stolen car. The clothes came from Jason James, and in March 2002 he and Daniel Whyte were arrested, convicted of the crime and sentenced to life imprisonment.

Guiseppe Martorana and his son, Stephen, who was 18 years old at the time of the murder. Stephen Martorana was shot in the chest during the robbery and still has a bullet lodged in his spine. His girlfriend, Isabella, was also shot and sustained serious internal injuries. The crime was solved when the analysis of paint traces found on Guiseppe's car were matched to a stolen getaway car.

TOXICOLOGY AND DRUGS

Drugs and toxic chemicals span a massive range, from alcohol, which is a socially acceptable drug, to those such as heroin and crack cocaine, which are universally frowned upon, and on to killers, including arsenic and ricin, that are used only as tools of aggression or suicide. Over their careers, most forensic toxicologists are called on to identify all these types of drugs.

Toxicology – the study of poisons and their effects – plays a part in forensics at three levels:

◆ A criminalist may be asked to see if a person's behaviour has been influenced by a drug.

◆ A forensic team may examine evidence to see whether a suspect has been manufacturing illicit compounds.

◆ Forensic experts will look for evidence that a toxic substance has killed a person.

ILLEGAL USE OF DRUGS

Estimates suggest that up to 34 percent of adults in the United Kingdom have used illicit drugs, with the highest proportion being addicted to alcohol, a mood-altering drug that's illegal in situations where consumption could be dangerous, for example when a person is at work or in charge of

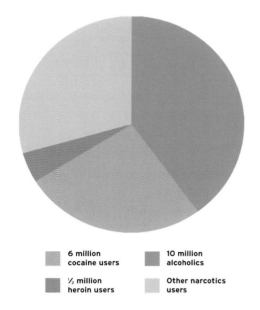

6 million
cocaine users

10 million
alcoholics

½ million
heroin users

Other narcotics
users

Chart to show, out of an estimated 23 million drug-users in the US, the proportions addicted to each drug type.

machines or vehicles. The size of the problem is reflected in the criminalist's workload: up to 75 percent of the work going through a forensic service laboratory may be related to drugs.

Selling illegal drugs such as heroin and cocaine is big business, and vast fortunes have been made by those involved in the trade. The amount of money at stake encourages people to go to extreme lengths, including violence, to protect their interests. For the evidence gatherers at drug-related crime scenes, there's the obvious task of looking for stashes of tablets, powders or blocks of resin, as well as searching for the signs of drug use such as needles and syringes, or in some cases the paraphernalia of drug manufacture. But evidence isn't just left lying around. Often the more important evidence is a part of the victim or suspect.

When someone inhales, ingests or injects a drug, it moves into his or her bloodstream and circulates around the body. Therefore, taking and analysing a blood sample can be one way of capturing evidence of use. To have a good chance of tracking down drugs, a forensic specialist needs about 10 millilitres of blood, though some of the newer test procedures

Toxicologists perform screening tests on blood to check for the presence of drugs.

can now work on smaller samples. Urine is also a good sample to search through, as the body sends to the bladder many of the chemicals it would rather not have floating around.

One of the problems faced by any toxicologist is that drugs don't just enter the body, perform their action, and then leave in the person's urine. The body's biochemical machinery normally alters a drug's molecules while it remains in the body. This means that a toxicologist spends most of his time looking for chemical byproducts that indicate that a drug has been used, rather than searching for the drug itself.

IDENTIFYING ILLICIT COMPOUNDS

Two sets of tests are normally used in deciding what drug is present in any sample. The first is a set of screening tests aimed at reducing the possibilities and pointing to a few likely candidates. The second is a range of tests aimed at confirming exactly what the suspicious substance is.

Screening

Some of the simplest screening tests look for a specific colour change when part of the evidence is placed in a known solution:

◆ Drop **heroin** or **morphine** in a mixture of formaldehyde and sulphuric acid and the liquid turns purple.

◆ The same solution turns orange-brown with **amphetamines.**

◆ Add some dilute cobalt acetate to some methanol and pour this over the sample before topping up with a little isopropylaine mixed with methanol, and the solution will turn violet-blue if a **barbiturate** was present.

◆ **LSD** can be detected by a solution, containing the chemical p-dimethylaminobenzaldehyde in hydrochloric acid and ethyl alcohol, turning blue-purple. The test is often difficult to perform at a crime scene, because LSD is used in such small quantities.

◆ A three-stage test can show whether a powder contains **cocaine.** Add the powder to cobalt thiocyanate dissolved in water and glycerine, and the solution turns blue. Pour in some hydrochloric acid and it now turns pink. Finally, if after adding chloroform the solution turns blue again just in the chloroform layer, the sample contains cocaine.

Confirming

Growing crystals is another way of identifying the chemicals contained in a powder. Experts simply dissolve a small quantity of the sample in a drip of carefully selected liquid placed on a microscope slide – and wait. In a few hours, the drug starts to appear in the form of crystals, which have a highly characteristic shape. In many cases the reason for the distinctive shape is not known, but that's unimportant. So long as the person examining the crystals has enough experience, he or she will be able

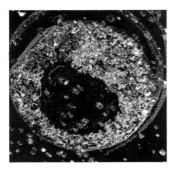

Formation of arsenic crystals viewed under a light micrograph.

to tell investigators all they need to know. The problem with most forensic drug evidence is that the sample is not pure. The active drug is likely to be either not particularly highly refined or deliberately mixed with some diluting agent. To get around this, a forensic laboratory often performs some form of chromatography on it, and compares the results with reference samples that they have carried out with known ingredients. The ultimate test is probably to combine gas chromatography with mass spectrometry. The process of chromatography separates the sample into individual ingredients, and the mass spectrometer smashes these into little pieces and analyses what comes out, giving a reading that is highly specific for individual compounds.

SPOTTING KILLER CHEMICALS

When death by poisoning is suspected, investigators can be much more invasive than is possible with living victims. A pathologist who specialises in legal work (a forensic pathologist) performs an autopsy and passes over a sizeable mass of tissue and other samples to the lab. These samples may include the entire stomach contents, half the person's liver, both kidneys, all the urine from the bladder, and half the brain.

The pathologist also collects blood from the right and left chambers of the heart, as well as from other sites around the body. On top of this, the spleen is sent for testing if there is any suspicion that cyanide was involved, because cyanide particularly affects this organ.

If arsenic poisoning is suspected, the forensic lab can work on an almost entirely decomposed body, because arsenic can be detected in hair, nails and bone – body parts that survive decomposition.

If alcohol is thought to be connected with a death, toxicologists need to take particular care with blood taken from the corpse. This is because there's a real possibility that bacteria, which multiply within a decomposing body, could produce ethyl alcohol, and this could affect any measures of alcohol levels.

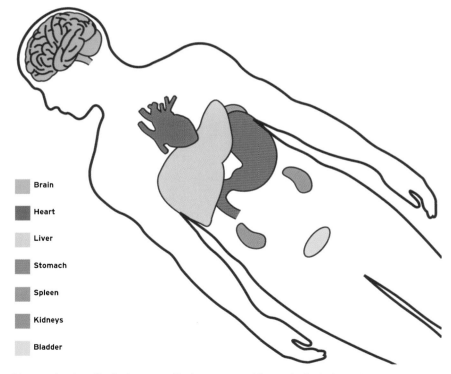

Brain

Heart

Liver

Stomach

Spleen

Kidneys

Bladder

Diagram to show the body organs that are removed for analysis during autopsy. Certain organs show up the presence of foreign materials, such as poisons, better than others.

FOILING THE PERFECT MURDER

A murder by poisoning that leaves no trace is more often a feature of fiction than fact. This is partly because most poisons produce clearly defined symptoms and chemical analysis can then track down the agent. There's also a huge element of uncertainty involved in giving poisons – a dose of chemical that could kill one person within minutes could leave another totally unaffected – potentially wrecking the poisoner's plan.

However, if the doctor who signs a death certificate is not trained to look for signs of poisoning and sees no reason for suspecting murder, he could easily overlook tell-tale symptoms. Poison can be the perfect weapon.

In trying to work out whether toxins are present, some basic chemistry is very useful. Some drugs, such as barbiturates, are acidic; others, such as amphetamines and methadone, are alkaline. If you add some acid to the sample, then acidic compounds are less likely to remain dissolved in solution. Add some chloroform to this mixture, shake it, and the acidic compounds will move into the chloroform in preference to the watery acid. Let it stand for a minute or two and the chloroform will separate from the water, carrying the compound with it, and leaving behind many other chemicals. Conversely, adding alkaline solutions to a sample will enable a toxicologist to go after any alkaline compounds.

Above: American doctor Arthur Warren Waite was convicted of the murder of Mr and Mrs Peck, in 1916. He poisoned the couple using bacteria from genuine diseases, in an effort to avoid suspicion.

Right: Dr Hawley Harvey Crippen, an American-born physician who poisoned his wife in 1910 and buried her body in the cellar of his London home.

Toxicologists can be called in when a body is found in a fire. If the person died from smoke inhalation, there should be tell-tale signs in the blood. If the person had been murdered beforehand, and the fire started to cover the murderer's tracks, the victim won't have had a chance to inhale the cocktail of chemicals usually present in smoke. In this case, it would be time to take a long hard look for signs of violence.

When investigating cases of death or ill health, toxicologists may not always be looking for a determined killer. Toxic chemicals occasionally arise in industrial leaks or factory explosions. On these occasions, the laboratory may be looking to find evidence of how far the toxic chemical has spread, or trying to work out how many people have been affected.

SEROLOGY

The term "serology" refers to the study of body fluids. Often these fluids are blood and semen, but the tests can also look at saliva and sweat. Faecal matter fits into this category, because its mucus coating may contain evidence. These fluids are important because they all contain cells from the person who made it, and these are important because, biologically speaking, each cell is a miniature version of you. If you can interrogate the cell, you can find valuable information about the original owner.

DOES RED EQUAL DEAD?

A large red stain or a red jelly-like substance is found. While the first assumption is that this is a person's blood, there are three basic questions that need asking in sequence:

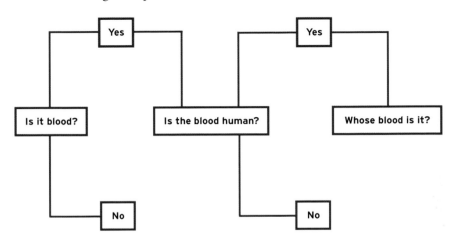

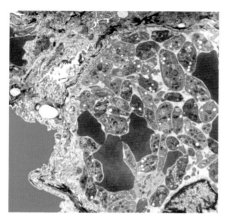

Forensic investigators use a variety of chemicals to differentiate between human blood and other substances that look similar.

Is it blood?

Blood from all living creatures shares many basic similarities that enable a forensic expert to check a stain and quickly see if it's the work of an attacker or a prankster.

The expert may drop a small piece of stained evidence in a solution and look for a colour change. If you mix phenolphthalein with hydrogen peroxide nothing happens, but add a little blood and the solution rapidly turns pink. This occurs because blood contains peroxidase, an enzyme that rapidly breaks down hydrogen peroxide, and the phenolphthalein responds to this reaction.

One important thing about this test is that enzymes can operate at very low concentrations, so you need only a tiny amount of peroxidase in the sample to get a reaction. In other words, if done carefully this test will work on an item that has a remarkably small amount of blood.

Another blood-finding method also depends on peroxidase. This method can be used at a crime scene where, say, a violent death is thought to have occurred but no bloodstains can be seen (perhaps because the suspect cleaned the area before police arrived). Forensic scientists spray a special mixture of chemicals, called luminol, onto a large area and turn out the lights. The luminol causes a chemical reaction with the peroxidase, and glows wherever there is blood. The test is very sensitive. Even if bloodstains are diluted 300,000 times – a very thorough wash – luminol will still work. As well as its ability to track down blood, luminol has another advantage. It doesn't damage the evidence. Once luminol has done its job, an expert can lift the trace of blood on a saline-soaked cotton swab and take it away for further analysis.

Is the blood human?

The body has a remarkable way of fighting infections that a forensic scientist can harness and put to use. When a foreign protein, such as a bacterium or virus, enters the body it generates antibodies. These stick to the foreigners, and enable the body to destroy them. This sticking is highly specific. A particular type of antibody will only stick to one type of protein. Scientists have developed ways of building their own antibodies targeted at a huge range of substances that they are interested in searching for. Some lock onto human blood, and can be used to check that a bloodstain did actually come from a human. Others lock onto blood from dogs, horses, sheep or just about any animal you could think of. This means that scientists can say exactly what sort of living creature created the blood that left the stain.

These immunoassays are not just limited to testing what type of animal lost some of its blood, and they are not just limited to searching thorough a blood sample. One well-used antibody looks for THC-9-carboxylic acid, the chemical that turns up in a person's urine if they smoke marijuana. In this case, the antibody will still find trace evidence up to 10 days after a person has smoked the drug.

Whose blood is it?

Finding blood is all well and good, but unless you can say who it came from you are not much further forward.

At the beginning of the twentieth century, Austrian scientist Karl Landsteiner discovered that blood can be classified into a number of distinct groups. Landsteiner's work had an immediate impact on general medicine, as it explained that only certain blood groups were compatible with certain others.

Later, determining a bloodstain's group became a routine part of forensic medicine. Although many people share the same blood group, police could nevertheless use blood analysis to narrow their hunt for a

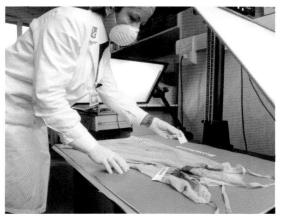

suspect considerably. For example, if blood left behind by a burglar was found to be group A, and a suspect's blood was group AB, then that suspect could be eliminated from the investigation.

Over the decades, more and more features were found in the composition of blood that varied between

An item of blood-stained evidence from a murder investigation is labelled in preparation for photography.

individuals. Comparing a whole series of factors made blood analysis a much more powerful tool.

Recent years have, however, seen blood groups lose some of their importance, thanks to the scientific importance of DNA analysis. As we will discover in chapter nine, by testing features of the DNA found in blood, scientists can produce a "genetic fingerprint" that most experts believe is as unique to an individual as a traditional fingerprint. This test is not only very powerful, but is also quick to perform and only needs tiny samples of blood.

SEXUAL ATTACK

The coded sequences in the arrangements of this DNA profile are unique to every individual. This is also known as a genetic fingerprint.

Collecting evidence in a situation where a person claims they have been raped or sexually assaulted is a particularly sensitive issue. If the allegation is correct, the victim has just been through a traumatic and highly intimate ordeal. Now, specially trained police officers are about to ask the person to go through another intimate examination so that they can recover any evidence that may be left behind. Accusing someone of rape is a serious charge, so courts demand a high level of evidence before they will convict.

Owing to the physical violence that is part of a sexual assault, there's every chance that blood will have transferred from the attacker to the victim. Traces of semen are also often found on the victim or her clothing. Consequently swab samples are taken from any region of the body where the victim claims that sexual contact occurred. And if the victim says the attacker bit, kissed or licked her, then that part of her body is swabbed particularly carefully, because DNA techniques could well recover a genetic fingerprint from this activity. Experts will need a 7 millilitre sample of the victim's blood to rule out any blood smears that have come from her.

On top of this, there's every chance that a forensic specialist could find some of the attacker's hair, or fibres from the attacker's clothing clinging to the victim. Scraping under the victim's fingernails can also be particularly productive, as there could easily be a mass of the attacker's cells if the victim fought back during the assault.

Finally, the forensic investigator collects at least 30 millilitres of the victim's urine so that the forensic laboratory can look for evidence of a "date-rape" drug.

It may be that the person accused has been detained, in which case investigators will be very keen to examine his clothing for reciprocating evidence. The most valuable item will probably be the suspect's underwear. If a penetrative sexual attack has occurred, there's a good chance that DNA techniques will be able to find traces of the victim's DNA on this garment.

Locating a patch of semen can often be a matter of searching for a suspicious dry, crusty mark. But looking for small spots can be harder. Now, forensic experts have to introduce a bit of science. Semen does not just contain sperm, but is also loaded with biological molecules that help sperm make it to the egg. One of these molecules, acid phosphatase, can be detected using what's known as the acid phosphate test. A forensic technician lightly rubs a moistened piece of filter paper over the suspected area, picking up any traces of semen on the paper. Then a drop of acidic sodium naphthylphosphate and Fast Blue B dye is placed on the paper. If the paper picked up some acid phosphatase, the dye will turn purple – a positive result. Now microscopic analysis may be used to locate sperm, or DNA techniques used to collect genetic material. Either way, confirming the presence of semen will strengthen the prosecution's case.

BLOOD SPATTER ANALYSIS

Blood can tell you more than simply whose veins it used to flow through. The pattern of the stain can determine where a person was when the blood escaped, and whether he or she was alive or dead at the time.

A blood spatter will often be formed of a blob with a fine tail at one side. This pattern indicates that the blood was travelling fast when it hit the object and the tail will point in the direction it came from. Experts can work out from which direction the blood struck the object. If the stain is circular, blood struck the object straight on; if the stain is egg-shaped, blood came from an angle, and the greater the angle, the more elongated the stain will be. If the blood has travelled at great speed, say, propelled by a bullet, then the droplet will be surrounded by myriad smaller flecks. A smeared bloodstain tells you that someone rubbed against it. That person will be carrying a stain, probably on a trouser leg or coat. Trails of blood can show how an incident developed, and how people moved from place to place. Quite often both the victim and assailant will lose blood at a crime scene, so it's important to determine whose blood makes up each separate mark. A large pool of blood shows that the person was alive in that spot for some time after receiving a wound; dead bodies stop bleeding quickly when the heart stops pumping blood around the body. If the spatter marks are very clear, you can learn a great deal about the weapon used. When someone stabs or beats a person to death, the killer does not swing the weapon in a straight line, but rather in a curve, and the direction of the curve shows whether the weapon had been held in the left or right hand. A narrow track of blood suggests that something fine, such as a sharp knife, had been used, while a broad band of blood spatters could suggest something more like a baseball bat. These marks also give clues about how frenzied the attack had been, and how many blows the killer gave. Finally, an area of floor with no blood can be just as revealing as the rest of a blood-spattered scene. Obviously something had stood there during the attack. It may be that the shape of that clear space could match an important box, bag or container that has been taken away by the killer.

FINGERPRINTS

No two fingerprints belonging to a single person are alike, and no two people share the same prints. Moreover, a person's prints are permanent throughout life; record them at birth and you'll be able to spot the same person when they die of old age. These facts have made fingerprinting an extremely important tool in crime detection.

THE HISTORY AND DEVELOPMENT OF FINGERPRINTING

1856 A chance observation led the way to the use of fingerprints in fighting crime. Sir William Herschel, chief magistrate of Jungipoor, India, asked people to make an imprint of their hand or fingers on the contracts they signed. The idea was that the personal contact with the document would instill a greater concept of ownership. It wasn't long, though, before Herschel began to see that each fingerprint was unique.

1880 A Scottish physician, Henry Fauld, published an article in the international science journal *Nature* suggesting that fingerprints could be used as a practical means of identification.

1883 Fingerprinting caught people's imagination and the author Mark Twain published *Life on the Mississippi*, in which a murderer is identified by his prints. But there had to be some way to classify them if they were to have forensic power. Searching through hundreds of suspects' prints looking for one that matches the crime scene evidence would be an impossible task.

1891 An Argentinian police official, Juan Vucetich, developed the first criminal fingerprint ID system, which was used to convict a murderer in the following year. His system is still used in Spanish-speaking countries.

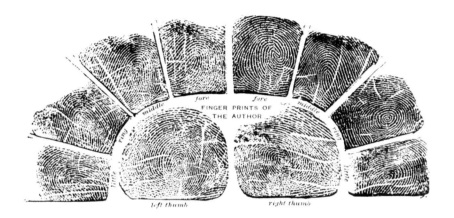

An example of early fingerprinting from the book *Fingerprints* by Sir Francis Galton. The prints shown are his own. Galton was responsible for the classification system of fingerprints as a means of identifying criminals.

1892 Francis Galton published *Fingerprints*, which established a system of classification for prints, known as Galton's Details. His ideas underpin most currently used systems. Importantly, Galton also calculated that the chance of any two people sharing a common print was one in 64 billion.

1897 English-speaking regions inherited a fingerprinting system developed by Englishman Sir Edward Henry. Much of Henry's work built on ideas of Francis Galton. Henry separated fingerprints into those with whorls and those with loops and arches. He assigned different values to each characteristic. Any fingers with arches or loops have a value of zero, but those with whorls were given a higher value, which varied according to which finger the whorl was on.

Fingers are paired as in the table below, and a whorl on the first pair of fingers is given a value of 16, the second pair is given 8, the third gets 4, the fourth 2, and the fifth 1. These pairs are then treated as fractions, and the fractions added up, including a value of 1 on the top and bottom of the fraction. Take, for example, a person with a whorl on their right ring finger and left index finger. The value for the left hand is 9 (0 + 8 + 0 + 0 + 0 + 1), that for the right is 3 (0 + 0 + 0 +2 + 0 + 1). This person would have their fingerprint records placed in category 9/3.

16	8	4	2	1
Right index	Right ring	Left thumb	Little middle	Left little
Right thumb	Right middle	Right little	Left index	Left ring

Henry's code, which is still used today, generates 1,024 possible variations, and any individual's prints can be quickly sorted into one of these categories. This doesn't pinpoint a person – particularly as around 25 percent of people fall into category 1/1 – but even so it could massively reduce the number of suspects that police had to track down. It has proved particularly useful for spotting criminals working under false names, as their prints matched those given under previous aliases.

Classification systems allow fingerprint experts to place a person's print in a group of similar prints. They then just have to search for specific features that will be unique to an individual. This could include the way that a scar cuts across a print, as well as noting the places that ridges start and finish, or where they join and split. One of the obvious limitations, however, is that a record of all 10 fingerprints is needed.

1902 The first systematic use of fingerprinting to aid in criminal identification was made by the New York Civil Service Commission.

1911 Thomas Jennings became the first person in the US to be convicted on the basis of fingerprint evidence. It appears that Jennings had murdered someone called Charles Hiller while committing a burglary.

Categories of print

At a crime scene, prints fall into one of three broad categories, depending on how easy it is to see them:

Patent prints

Patent prints can be seen by just looking and perhaps made because the person's hand was covered in something like ink, oil or blood, and the mark is clearly visible. To collect one of these, a criminalist often simply needs to take a careful close-up photograph.

Latent prints

This type of fingerprint cannot be seen until you have enhanced them with a powder or chemical reagent.

Impressed prints

These are prints that have been pressed in a soft material such as the surface of a congealed pool of blood or perhaps mud or snow. Forensics experts may be able to capture impressed prints by photographing them, or by casting a moulding.

GETTING THE PERFECT PRINT

Getting a latent print takes time and practise.
A fingerprint examiner uses delicate brushes, some with natural bristles or camel hair, others with feathers or fibreglass, to gently layer powder over a print. Dusting powders of various different types and colours are the classic means of making latent prints visible. Some powders are fluorescent and are useful on multicoloured surfaces, as the print can be made to shine in UV light, while the rest of the surface appears black.

Step 1. Prints are so fragile that even the softest brush could destroy them. The fingerprint examiner gently shakes or twirls the brush just above where the print is thought to be. Once it starts to come into view, the examiner builds up layers of dust, each time moving the brush in the direction of the lines in the print. Excess dust is cleared with compressed air. Hopefully, a clear print now needs to be preserved.

Step 2. The print is photographed and lifted onto a card. Lifting tape may be used for single prints. This process needs a steady hand, because the tape must be placed straight down on the print without wrinkles or bubbles. The tape needs to be pulled away in one long smooth movement

and carefully laid on a card. Each print is given a number. The location of the print is also recorded, in the form of a description and as a map or diagram of the scene. Sometimes there may be enough dust left in the print that the expert can repeat this process and lift it for a second time. The advantage is that this second lift may give a clearer view of certain details within the print.

Step 3. On some surfaces, a print is so fragile that it has to be stabilised before it can be enhanced with dust. Experts often use the cyanoacrylic chemicals in superglue for this purpose. A small hood is first placed over the print. Then some superglue is heated to about 120°F (60°C), so that it boils and the fumes waft over the print. Chemicals in the fumes stick to the molecules that form the print. This process not only makes the print more noticeable, but also gives a perfect surface for fingerprint dust to stick to.

Step 4. Examiners spend most of their time searching for prints on objects, but sometimes they need to take prints from dead bodies (live suspects are normally printed in a police station), either at the scene or during an autopsy. Getting prints from a dead body can be difficult. If the person has recently died, rigor mortis makes their muscles clench. After a few hours the muscles relax, and an expert can straighten the hand and get a set of prints. Taking prints from a body that has been in water for some time can be difficult as the deceased's skin often peels off. In this case, a technician may have to wrap the person's skin around their own finger to get a print.

NEW TECHNOLOGY

In the days before computerisation, the information gleaned from fingerprints was kept on individual cards in the form of vast filing systems. Finding a match between a print from a crime scene and anyone on file was time-consuming, as investigators would have to sift through thousands of cards. Even though there are ways to narrow the search, with the cards being sorted by such characteristics as sex, age, presence of scars, presence of whorl, loop and arch formations in various fingers, and ridge counts and tracings, you might at best have found that you have a quarter of the cards to sort through, rather than the entire fingerprint filing system. Computers have vastly sped up the search process. Current systems can perform 40,000 searches each day if necessary.

Computerised fingerprint systems now scan prints picked up at crime scenes and automatically plot the relative positions of features such as the places where ridges divide in two. They also note the angle between different ridges. Once this data is stored numerically it is easy for the computer to search its database looking for potential matches. It's then down to a fingerprint expert to scrutinise the prints from possible suspects to see if the computer got it right.

This computerised analysis has another advantage besides speed. It can work on the assortment of partial prints often recovered from a crime scene. After all, no criminal deliberately leaves a full set of prints behind, so police often have to work with marks that are partially smudged or on small surfaces that are too small to contain a whole print.

The next step in the technological assistance to crime fighting is, wherever possible, to do away with paper and cards altogether. A suspect called in for questioning will place his fingers on a scanner pad, and the computer will create a digital image of the print, then use specialised

If investigators suspect that latent prints are on evidence collected from a crime scene, they will dust the item with fluorescent powder and view it under ultraviolet light.

image analysis to search for identifying features. This image and the accompanying analysis can be stored in a computer, used to check against existing records, and sent to any police force in the world at the click of a mouse. It's this sort of electronic fingerprint that has being incorporated into some biometric security systems; paper records are on their way out.

Some are concerned, however, with the advent of computerised fingerprinting, that the palm database will not be as carefully maintained. Palm prints are as important identifiers as fingerprints, as they have eight to ten times more minutiae than fingerprints. Palm-print scanners are being refined for common usage but this technology is more difficult because of the many contours on the hand. The storage of a larger file is also a concern. There is no doubt that these new technologies will make solving crimes easier, but it is a matter of time before they are cost-effective and therefore widely used.

THE BODY IN A SUITCASE

A man walking along a country lane in Yorkshire one November morning in 2001 spotted a suitcase. Inside was an almost naked body of a woman. Her face had been bound with tape.

Police had very little information to go on. First impressions were that the woman was of Asian origin, probably from East Asia rather than India or Pakistan, but dental examinations, DNA profiling and recovering her fingerprints failed to identify her. When the information was sent to Interpol there was more luck. Her details matched those of a Korean missing person listed on a Southeast Asian website.

The Korean government holds fingerprints of all its citizens. British police used this data to identify the victim as Hyo Jung Jin, a 21-year-old student at Lyon University, France. She had come to London on a sightseeing trip and had disappeared almost immediately, but not before emailing her friend in Korea to say she had met a new man.

Police were quick to link her death with that of a second Korean student. In March 2002, the body of In Hea Song was found hidden in a concealed cupboard at a London address. Both Jin and Song appeared to have suffocated. The landlord of the property was 31-year-old Soo Kyo Kim.

Investigators soon found a roll of tape at the property that was similar to that used to bind Jin. It turned out that this was a very unusual roll as it was sold almost exclusively from one outlet. Furthermore, only 2,000 rolls had ever been made and only 851 had been sold. Police also

The identity of Hyo Jung Jin remained a mystery until the Korean government's fingerprint database identified her as a Korean student missing from Lyon University, France.

found that blue paint on one corner of the suitcase matched paint on one of the bedroom walls at Kim's address. They discovered Jin's blood on skirting boards, walls, the edge of a divan bed and on the carpet, as well as in the trunk of a Peugeot Kim had hired in October 2001.

Prosecuting officials used evidence from a property in Canada where Kim had been staying to link him to the body in the cupboard. Miss Song had been gagged and bound with the tape. Orange paint found on a T-shirt taken from a house in Toronto matched paint found on the tape used to bind her wrists. DNA taken from the T-shirt matched Kim, linking all three elements together. In addition, property in the cupboard with Miss Song was linked by DNA to Miss Jin.

Soo Kyo Kim was tried and found guilty of the murders of both women, thanks to a trail of evidence that started with fingerprint analysis.

DNA ANALYSIS

Recent years have seen crime detection revolutionised by DNA analysis, or genetic fingerprinting, the most powerful technique of identifying individuals. DNA analysis helps solve previously baffling crimes, and allows those who have been wrongly imprisoned to prove their innocence.

DNA, or deoxyribonucleic acid, is the code-carrying molecule found in the centre of almost all cells. It's packaged in 46 chromosomes that are stored inside a cell's nucleus. Under an electron microscope DNA is an incredibly long and fine strand of material – around 6 feet (2 metres) of it coils inside each cell.

DNA stores information – about cell formation, growth and reproduction – and holds it in a form that cells find easy to duplicate. Both of these features make it valuable for forensic scientists. DNA is constructed using four different building blocks, which scientists call "bases". The information is stored in a code created by the sequence of these bases. It is in effect a four-letter language, and the DNA inside each human cell consists of about 3 billion bases.

While much of our DNA is used to tell the body how to build and function itself, there are large stretches of "junk" DNA that don't appear to have any particular function. The lengths of these regions of junk DNA vary between different people, and forms a unique genetic fingerprint for each individual. But just as a normal fingerprint doesn't give a picture of a person, a genetic fingerprint does not tell you anything about their genes. It is, however, a marker that can link evidence with a specific person.

INSIDE FORENSICS

RUNNING A DNA TEST

1. A sample of human cells is needed to run a DNA test. Blood or body tissue found at a crime scene or semen collected from a rape victim are obvious examples, but some DNA sources may be less apparent. Using lab techniques to amplify a sample's amount of genetic material, scientists can work with minute quantities of material. A telephone receiver, an envelope's seal, the rim of a used glass, or a discarded cigarette butt can contain enough cells for a scientist to examine.

2. DNA is extracted from a cell's nucleus using a salt solution, or a mixture of chloroform and phenol.

3. DNA is multiplied in a process called the polymerase chain reaction (PCR). A DNA molecule is like a spiralling ladder. The DNA is heated, splitting the "rungs" of the ladder and leaving two half-ladders. When the DNA cools, a new set of DNA building blocks will rebuild the missing sides of each half-ladder. Within a matter of minutes you have two new strands of DNA. Heat and cool again and you can go from two to four strands. A third cycle will create eight and a fourth 16. Each cycle takes as little as 20 minutes, so it's easy to see how a scientist can quickly make copies of the original genetic data.

4. By a little bit of technical wizardry, scientists can manipulate this process so that they increase only the number of copies of the regions of DNA whose length varies between different people, and leave the rest basically untouched. Now the DNA just needs to be analysed.

DNA dabs

A sample of DNA is loaded on to an agarose gel for separation by electrophoresis.

Scientists use a process called electrophoresis to separate the different variable regions and create a visual record of these. They place a sample of DNA in a small well cut into the surface of a gel spread over the top of a plate, and then apply an electrical current across the plate. DNA molecules naturally have a small negative charge on them, so the current can drag the fragments of DNA through the gel. The greater the charge on the DNA fragment, the faster it will travel, but smaller fragments meet least resistance and so travel faster than large ones. As each fragment of DNA will have a unique combination of charge, each will reach different places on the plate.

The result is a gel with a series of bars of DNA fragments in a line. Using a few chemicals allows scientists to see where the DNA is on the plate, and generate an image that looks a little like a badly constructed ladder. The spacing of the bars is unique for an individual person, just as each pattern of whorls on a fingerprint is unique, and so the image has become known as a "genetic fingerprint".

WHAT DNA DOESN'T TELL YOU

Genetic fingerprints have become very controversial. Bio-statisticians argue about exactly how many variable regions need to be examined before we can be sure that no two people will share the same set. This is very important, because members of juries are easily swayed by an expert saying that a suspect's genetic fingerprint matches DNA found on a piece of evidence; this one piece of information can lead them to dismiss all

DNA and the human genome

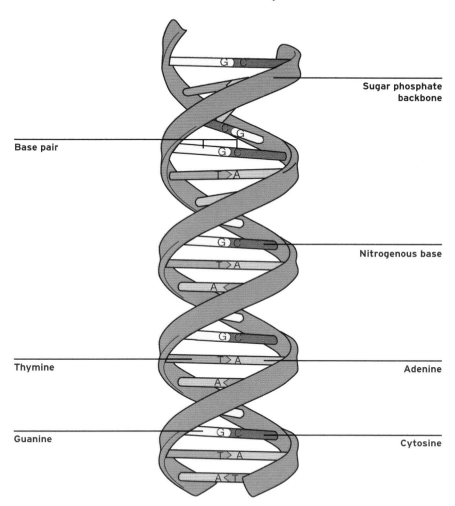

A strand of DNA, showing how the nucleotides
link together to create the double helix formation.

DNA sequence with four strips representing adenine, guanine, cytosine and thymine.

other evidence and alibis. Also, just as a fingerprint is very different to a portrait, so too a DNA fingerprint says almost nothing about the person – it just happens that it's unique. It may be that in the future, DNA analysis will become so fast and cheap that investigators will be able to look at samples found at a crime scene and then search for specific information in the code-carrying region of the chromosomes that will show them the person's distinguishing features, such as hair colour and stature. But for the moment that lies within the realms of science fiction.

The ability of DNA analysis to come to conclusions based on minuscule samples is also a problem. Because a single hair is found at a site doesn't necessarily mean that the person was there. Just think how many hairs you must lose in a normal day at work or in public places. Imagine if one of these found its way to a crime scene, and you wound up in the dock explaining that you weren't involved. Evidence from DNA must be treated like all other evidence – it's useful, but needs corroboration from other sources.

MULTIPLE USES

While DNA evidence has been a powerful tool to catch criminals, it doesn't stop there. It can also identify the father of a child in a paternity dispute, because half of the genetic information in a child comes from the father. Analysing the father and child will show if there are similarities in their DNA. If the child in question is a boy, then you can compare the Y chromosomes of both individuals, as this package of DNA only comes from the father. Investigators also use genetic fingerprinting to try to establish the identity of victims in situations where bodies have been reduced to small, jumbled pieces, as happened as a result of the terrorist attacks on September 11, 2001. And it is not just used on humans. DNA profiles can also be used to identify specific bacteria or viruses. This helped US scientists pinpoint the source of the bacteria in the anthrax attacks that caused so much fear and disruption in 2001, though this information alone was not enough to track down the person who sent it.

MEGADATABASES

One of the beauties of a DNA fingerprinting is that information can be easily stored in a computer. Countries around the world are creating huge databases that record DNA from crime sites, convicted criminals and, in some cases, members of the public.

The United States

The FBI laboratory's Combined DNA Index System (CODIS) has become an effective tool for solving violent crimes. CODIS enables federal, state and local crime labs to exchange and compare DNA profiles electronically. Police can therefore use it to link crimes to each other, as well as to point them toward specific suspects. CODIS began as a small-scale project in 1990, but the DNA Identification Act of 1994 allowed the FBI to set up a national DNA law enforcement index. By 2003, all 50 states had laws requiring police to place DNA profiles of certain offenders on the CODIS database. By this point CODIS held just under 1.5 million profiles of convicts, as well as over 66,000 profiles of DNA found on physical evidence collected at numerous crime scenes.

THE CASE OF EDWARD HONAKER

On the morning of June 23, 1984, Angela Nichols and her boyfriend at the time, Samuel Dempsey, were sleeping in their car on the roadside in rural Virginia, USA. An armed man, pretending to be a police officer approached them, ordered them out of the car and forced Dempsey to go off into the woods. The assailant then kidnapped Nichols, drove off to a secluded area, and repeatedly raped her. Nichols reported that over the course of her ordeal her attacker had held the gun in his left hand and talked at length about his Vietnam War experience. She also initially told the police that she couldn't see her attacker clearly throughout the ordeal. Despite this, the police compiled a sketch of the attacker with the help of the victims.

One hundred miles away, another woman was raped and told the police that her attacker resembled her neighbour, Edward Honaker. Honaker had an alibi and was not charged with this attack, but the investigating office showed Honaker's picture to Nichols and Dempsey. They then picked Honaker's picture out of a photo line-up and proceeded to identify Honaker in court. Other evidence consisted of the truck that Honaker drove being similar to that of the attacker, camouflage clothing found at Honaker's house that was similar to that of the assailant, and most convincingly the testimony of a state forensic expert who claimed he had definitively matched a hair found on Nichols's shorts to Honaker.

Despite an alibi, corroborated by three others, Edward Honaker was convicted of seven counts of sexual assault, sodomy and rape and sentenced to three life sentences and 34 years.

Eventually, Honaker made contact with an organisation that works to free the wrongfully convicted and they discovered inconsistencies in the prosecution's case. Their investigation revealed that Nichols and Dempsey had been hypnotised at times and that their initial description of the assailant did not fit Honaker. In fact, Nichols and Dempsey did not identify Honaker at all until after their hypnosis sessions, and if Honaker's defence had been privy to this information, Nichols and Dempsey's identification would not have been admissible at trial, under Virginia law. Further it was also revealed that Honaker had undergone a vasectomy in 1976, a fact not known to the prosecution's witnesses and hardly brought up at trial, that Honaker was right-handed, and that he had never been to Vietnam. The organisation then proceeded to secure DNA testing on the biological evidence collected at Edward Honaker's case.

The prosecution's forensics experts had testified in the original trial that sperm was present in the semen on the vaginal swab. The prosecution contended that the sperm was Dempsey's but released the evidence to Honaker's lawyers. The test was further complicated by Nichols's claim of having a secret lover who could have contributed to the evidence.

DNA testing revealed that there were two different seminal deposits, one on Nichols's shorts and the other on the swab. However it categorically stated that even if Honaker were able to produce sperm, he was not the source of the sperm from either deposit. Dempsey and the second lover were also eliminated as the source of the sperm on the swab.

Based on this DNA evidence, Honaker filed for his convictions to be overturned. Edward Honaker was pardoned in 1994, having served 10 years of a sentence for a rape he did not commit. The state's forensics expert who testified about the matched hair on Nichols's shorts said that he would not have testified to the definitive match if he had known that Honaker had undergone a vasectomy.

The United Kingdom

In the UK, the National DNA Database grows at about 400,000 profiles a year. This rapid increase is largely due to the policy of taking samples from anyone arrested for even the most minor offences, and keeping them even if the person is not subsequently charged.

The theory behind this policy is that most major crimes are committed by people who have also committed minor offences. Civil liberties groups, however, are worried about this intrusion into people's lives, as well as being anxious about the misinterpretation of small fragments of DNA that may have arrived at a crime scene by chance.

This rapid rate of sample collection meant that at the beginning of 2003 there were over 2 million profiles recorded on the British database, and records of 180,000 samples that have been collected at various crime scenes.

Police are excited by how these records can be used to solve cases. In 2003, four out of 10 samples recovered from crime scenes instantly matched records in the database. Authorities claim that in a typical month the DNA database points the finger of suspicion at individuals in 15 murder cases, 31 rapes and 770 motor crimes.

INJUSTICE RESOLVED

Any useful forensic technique should be able to establish the truth, not simply gain a conviction. In other words, forensic science should be able to show that a suspect is innocent of the charges against him or her. Genetic fingerprinting is proving to be particularly good at doing this, and, thanks to DNA profiling, in recent years a number of convicts have had their cases repealed when genetic evidence showed that they had been wrongfully accused.

FORENSIC DATA

THE CASE OF STEPHEN COWANS

On January 23, 2004, Stephen Cowans walked out of the Suffolk Superior Court in Boston, Massachusetts, a free man and the 141st person in the United States to be exonerated as a result of post-conviction DNA testing.

Stephen Cowans had been found guilty of shooting and wounding an officer of the Boston Police Department on May 30, 1997. The evidence against him started with the wounded officer identifying him from a photo array, and then in July picking out Cowans in a line-up.

One other person and a family had seen the assailant. The single person had witnessed the attack from a second floor bedroom window and a family was present in a nearby home when the assailant stopped to drink from a glass of water. The witness from the second floor bedroom window also identified Cowans as the assailant, but did not identify Cowans from the line-up.

The assailant had also left a trail of belongings as he fled the scene — his baseball cap at the site of the shooting, and the weapon and his sweatshirt in the house where he took refuge. At the trial, prosecutors presented a fingerprint from the glass mug that experts claimed matched Cowans's left thumbprint. He was convicted of the crime in 1998.

In 2003, Stephen Cowans's defence team tested the DNA found on various items of evidence, including the glass mug that had the thumbprint, swabs taken from this mug, the baseball cap and the sweatshirt. There was no sign of Cowans's DNA. This prompted a re-examination of the thumbprint, and this time fingerprint experts said that it did not belong to Cowans. After a six-and-a-half-year prison sentence for a crime he didn't commit, Stephen Cowans walked free.

FIREARMS

Did a suspect use this gun to kill that person? Did these bullets come from that gun? Was it really self-defence? Is this a case of suicide or is foul play involved? These are some of the questions that forensic firearms experts are routinely asked.

Broadly speaking, you can divide firearms into two groups:
• Small handguns that can be held by either one or both hands.
• Larger shoulder firearms such as rifles and shotguns.

Shoulder-based weapons are more powerful and have greater accuracy than handguns.

There are also two different types of barrel:
• A **rifled barrel** has a set of gently spiralling grooves with edges that cut into the bullet as it chases along and makes it spin. This spinning allows the bullet to travel in a much straighter direction than would be possible without the spin and increases the gun's accuracy.
• A **smooth-bore barrel** weapon has no grooves and is consequently less accurate in the way they fire.

USE THE BULLET TO FIND THE CRIMINAL

The idea of linking a person to a crime by showing that he or she once held the gun has a long history. While performing an autopsy in 1794, a surgeon found a wad of paper buried in a bullet wound. Guns in those days were muzzle-loaders, and the wad would have been used to pack the

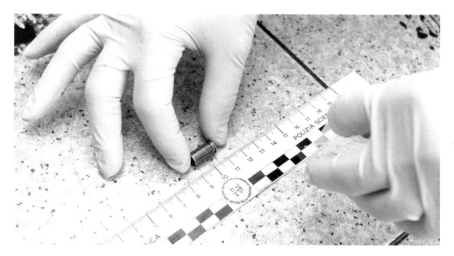

Measuring and recording a bullet cartridge at the scene of a crime. A shell case such as this can provide valuable evidence about the firearm used.

bullet and gunpowder into the gun before firing. When unfurled, the wad turned out to have been torn from a sheet of music. Later a suspect was arrested, and in his pocket was the rest of the same sheet of music. The man was soon hanging from the local gallows.

In modern guns, the ammunition consists of a bullet that is pointed at the front and a flat at the base. The base is held by a hollow shell case that is packed with gunpowder. In the rear of the case is a small amount of primer that ignites when the gun's firing pin dents the case. The bullet then flies off, and the shell case is held inside the gun or, in the case of some automatic loading systems, ejected.

Over the years forensic ballistics experts have developed an increasingly sophisticated battery of tests that enable them to link bullets with specific guns, and guns with people. Nowadays, many of these tests are computerised.

SCRAPING THE BARREL

Investigators hand over a gun and bullets found at a crime scene. Firearms experts are asked to say whether a particular gun was used in the crime. What process do they follow?

1. A new bullet is test-fired through the gun into a target filled with water or cotton wadding, capturing the bullet without damaging it. This newly fired bullet now bears the gun's signature of scratches. The expert scrutinises the markings on the bullet. When a bullet travels through a rifle barrel, the inside of the barrel scores a series of tiny scratches into it. The patterns of scratches are highly specific for particular types of gun, and are often sufficiently individual to link a bullet with a single weapon.

2. A comparison microscope is used to see if these marks match scratches on bullets found at the scene. The test bullet is examined and the most prominent set of scratches pinpointed. The other bullet is treated in the same way, the expert looking to see if the sets of scratches match.

3. Once the expert spots a possible match, he or she rotates both bullets in the same direction and at exactly the same rate to see if other markings come into view at the same time. If a low-power examination looks promising, the expert increases the magnification, and looks to see if smaller marks also line up.

4. It would be nice to think that this process is a precise science, but in reality there's a little art involved. No two bullets ever look exactly the

Observing the striations on a test bullet and one found at a crime scene, using a comparison microscope.

same. The bullet from the crime scene could have picked up additional markings when it struck the victim or anything else along the way. The gun barrel would present a different set of dust particles inside on each occasion it was fired, leaving differing marks on any bullet. Also, bullets themselves vary slightly in size, and so each will pick up its own unique set of marks as it travels down the barrel. It takes great expertise to conclude that two bullets almost certainly travelled down the barrel of one gun.

5. Useful information also comes from the shell case. The shape of the dent left by the firing pin on the shell case can vary from weapon to weapon, and examination can reveal a high probability that a particular gun was involved in a crime. In addition, when a gun fires, the explosion forces the shell case against the back of the chamber, and any imperfections in the chamber will become stamped into the shell. If the firearm was an automatic or semi-automatic weapon, the mechanism that loads and removes the shell will also leave characteristic marks. While this information is useful, it has less power than evidence found on the bullet – the fact that you have found a shell case linked to a gun at a crime scene does not in itself prove that a particular person was guilty of the offence.

RESIDUES

On many occasions gunpowder residues can yield valuable information. The pattern of residue can give a strong indication of how far the gun was from the target when the shot was fired. This sort of evidence can be useful if the suspect is claiming self-defence, as it will show how close he or she was to the victim. In cases of suspected suicide, careful examination shows highly characteristic patterns indicating that the weapon was held very close. The absence of these marks would raise deep suspicions of foul play.

These assessments have most use in court if the suspect's actual weapon can be used to produce a similar pattern of marks on a test surface. If investigators have not recovered a weapon, any comments will always have to be restricted to best guesses based on previous experience.

Bullet residues

Firing from less than $^3/_4$ of an inch (2 centimetres) leaves a heavy concentration of residue immediately around the bullet wound, and if the bullet has passed through clothing, the edges may be scorched or melted. Fabric can also be torn in a four-pointed star, created by gasses rushing back into the barrel immediately after the shot is fired. Holding the gun 12 to 16 inches (30 to 40 centimetres) away leaves scattered specks of burned and unburned powder, while shots fired from up to 3 feet (1 metre) away can leave traces of powder on the target.

An expert can still collect some residue even if the attacker was standing a mile or more away and using a high-powered rifle. This is because the bullet is coated with a small quantity of dust that is wiped off as it enters the victim and which can be collected by wiping carefully around the bullet's point of entry.

Swabbing a suspect's hand to gather gunshot residue and the presence of cordite which is often used in gun cartridges as a propellant. The most common site for collecting gunshot residue is the area between the fingers and thumb where the gun rests.

Shot residues

In the case of smooth-bore weapons that fire shot instead of individual bullets, the farther away a person was from the gun, the greater the spread of the shot. When held closer than about 6 feet (2 metres), the shot will be in one concentrated zone just a little wider in diameter than the gun's bore. As a rule of thumb, the diameter of the impact zone increases by about 1 inch (2.5 centimetres) for every additional 3 feet (1 metre) of separation.

Evidence doesn't only come from the victim. Swabbing a suspect's hands within a few hours of an offence, particularly the webbed region between thumb and forefinger, may detect chemical traces that will show whether he or she recently held or fired a gun. Ballistics experts then use neutron activation analysis or atomic absorption spectrophotometry to find traces of barium, lead and antimony, which are used in the primer. In some cases, a scanning electron microscope is used to show minuscule details, in which case samples are taken using specially made adhesive-coated aluminium discs. Different manufacturers of bullets use different gunpowder recipes when making up the explosive in each bullet.

INSIDE FORENSICS

HOW COMPUTERS LINK GUNS WITH CRIMES

As with so many areas of forensics, computers are increasingly helping criminalists. Law-enforcement agencies use powerful systems to examine individual bullets and compare them with previously recorded evidence stored in a database – in a fraction of the time it would take to do the same task without computers.

The FBI's DRUGFIRE database holds digitised images of cartridge cases. The integrated ballistic identification system (IBIS) developed for the US Bureau of Alcohol, Tobacco, Firearms and Explosives (ATF&E), carries digital images of both cartridges and bullets. In 1999, staff from the FBI and the ATF&E merged their two systems to create NIBIN, the National Integrated Ballistic Information Network. This drew together the individual strengths of each platform. The equipment allows firearms technicians to grab digital images of markings and let the computer make an initial search through the database. In seconds it can check against hundreds of thousands of records. The computer lists the most likely comparisons, and firearms examiners then check these.

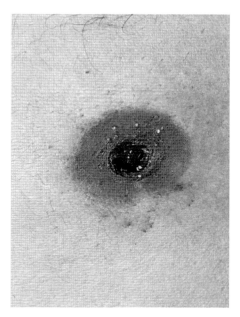

**Analysing a gunshot wound at an autopsy.
Note the soot residue around the bullet hole.**

Analysing the chemicals in the residue and comparing the results with a reference database may uncover the manufacturer of the offending bullet.

Interpreting the evidence is not a straightforward task. If there's no residue present on a person's hands, it could mean that they didn't fire the weapon, perhaps they wore a glove or the gun had a particularly clean firing action.

On the other hand, finding residue on a person's palm, but not between thumb and forefinger, may mean that the suspect picked up the gun after it had been fired, rather than pulling the trigger himself.

RECOVERING SERIAL NUMBERS

Every gun has its own serial number, which the authorities use to record ownership of individual weapons. Criminals often grind off these numbers to hide a firearm's original identity – but traces are sometimes left behind and the numbers can be restored.

When a number is stamped into a gun, the metal below each character is stressed, making it fractionally weaker than the surrounding area. With care, an expert can often use etching solutions, such as mixtures of hydrochloric acid and copper chloride, to dissolve this stressed metal, and re-establish the serial number. If revealed, the number is photographed immediately, as the etching process may continue and erase it completely.

TELLING THE STORY

A firearms investigator's first job at a crime scene is to try to work out how many shots were fired. It may be that witnesses can help by recalling the number of "bangs" they heard, and this can be confirmed if spent cartridges or bullets are found. Recovering the weapon is a huge step forward, and this too can give clues about the number of shots fired, as the number of unused cartridges still inside can be counted.

The next task is to find the bullets. Some of these may well be inside the victim, and taking X-ray images of his or her body will find them, or fragments of them. Often the bullets recovered from the scene of a crime are so badly squashed or mangled that markings aren't visible. Even so, locating the bullets can help investigators trace where the gun was when it was fired. Inserting rods or shining laser beams through bullet holes in furniture, walls, or any other item in the area can also help point toward the gun's location (see page 32). On occasions, forensic investigators may even make up a mannequin to represent the victim, complete with bullet holes that relate to his or her injuries. This can be particularly useful if more than one gun was involved and multiple shots were fired, as it can begin to show which shots were discharged from which weapon.

Discovering that a bullet ricocheted off the floor, walls or furniture can make a huge difference to any enquiry. It may be that the gun was facing away from the victim and fired accidentally, or as a warning shot with no intention of harming a person, but a sequence of chance bounces made it strike the victim. The defence team may well use this type of evidence to claim that a charge of manslaughter would be more appropriate than murder.

FORENSIC DATA

THE IMPORTANCE OF NIBIN

On June 2, 2000, a security guard was shot and killed in Houston, Texas. Investigators recovered a single .40 calibre bullet and a Smith and Wesson cartridge case. NIBIN linked this incident to an aggravated robbery that had occurred on May 20, 2000. The same gun had also been used in a robbery in which two shop clerks had been murdered. Looking through the records of incidents including .40 Smith and Wesson pistols, Houston PD's crime analysis units found an aggravated robbery on February 11, 2000, in which someone armed with this weapon stole a man's credit card.

Clearly this pistol was in the hands of a dangerous criminal. To track it down, investigators searched databases of stolen weapons and found the owner of one suitable candidate that had been reported as stolen a few months earlier. A spent cartridge provided by the owner matched the crime-scene evidence. Now they knew the weapon's make, model and serial number. Next they turned to the credit card. Someone had tried to use this after the robbery, but the transaction had been rejected. Even so, when police interviewed the shopkeeper they discovered that not only did he remember the occasion, he also knew the person who had tried to use the card, and in June 2000 two men were arrested and subsequently convicted. It had been a convoluted chase, but NIBIN had been invaluable.

MARKS AND IMPRESSIONS

Criminals put on gloves to avoid leaving fingerprints and wear masks to prevent cameras or witnesses recording their faces, but they can't avoid making marks on the ground. Their getaway cars inevitably leave behind some form of mark or impression, too.

A mark or impression is either a two-dimensional image on a flat surface, such as a footprint on a dusty wooden floor, or a three-dimensional impression such as a wheel-track in snow or mud.

Finding markings can be tricky, partly because first responders and investigators alike easily destroy them by accident. As a precaution against this, investigators work from the outer edges of the crime scene inward towards the centre. Markings can also be difficult to see if they are made on a hard surface.

Once a potential location of a marking is spotted, it is time to get out the brush and fingerprint powders. The task of enhancing a marking is often more difficult than with fingerprints, because unlike fingers, synthetic articles such as shoes and tyres do not leave behind oils and proteins to which dust easily adheres; they just rearrange the material they are on. Many of the criminalist's clever dyes and dusts won't help here.

Finding marks or prints

When marks or prints are found the investigator acts as follows:

1. A forensic photographer takes photos of the prints, placing a ruler in the shots so that size is recorded.

2. If the prints form a sequence, the distance between prints is measured to give clues about a person's height, as well as how fast he or she was moving. Even if the prints don't provide much detail, they can still be useful, as they may lead investigators toward areas of the crime scene that need to be given special attention.

3. If a tyre mark is found, criminalists look for the one from the opposite side of the vehicle. The distance between the two tracks and the width of each tread mark can indicate the sort of vehicle that created it.

4. Tool marks, such as those left after prizing open a window with a screwdriver, can also be moulded. This time the item will have to be taken back to the lab, as the impression is usually on a vertical surface and cannot be cast as it stands. When making relatively small casts it is best to insert the spatula used for stirring the cement into the material as it sets. This way it will become locked into the cast, giving both a handle and a label.

Footwear evidence can determine a certain make and size of shoe, and estimate the height of the wearer.

As with fingerprints, these markings can link different crimes together. Databases list prints from almost any article you can imagine – shoes, tyres, screws, you name it. These databases contain not only data from crime scenes, but also records of different manufacturers' products, so a shoeprint can easily reveal the make and size of the person's shoe, giving valuable additional information about just who investigators should be looking for.

DEEP PRINTS

Deep impressions made in materials such as mud, snow and sand can be very valuable to an investigation because they show high levels of detail. Technicians usually make casts of these deep prints as follows:

Getting prints in difficult circumstances

1. Place a box or ring around the print and pour in a ready-mixed casting material, such as dental cement, which sets quickly and records fine detail.

2. Before the cast has set completely the technician makes marks in the top of the cast that identify it and record its orientation.

3. A photograph is taken to show exactly where the cast was made, to record as much detail as possible and to help investigators paint a picture of events at the crime scene.

Water

Taking a print that is waterlogged can prevent an accurate cast being made. Unmixed dental cement is often used to absorb the water, then the cast is topped up with ready-mixed cement.

Environment

Inclement weather and the environment can thwart efforts to get information from deep prints. A footprint in sand will blow away unless dealt with quickly. Hair lacquer is often sprayed over the print to help bind it, thus giving time to pour a casting material into the print.

Snow

Tracks in snow are obviously prone to melting and so must be handled carefully. Snow itself can be stabilised a little with a material called Snow Print Wax, but the print will still need casting. Dental cement unfortunately takes longer to set when cold, and also gives out heat as it cures, but it's the only option. To try to get a good cast, the cement is used cold and poured in slowly to maximise the chance that the heat will dissipate through the snow without melting the print.

DIGITAL IMAGING

Police investigators call on computer power in some situations, for example, when they can't see a footprint on a relatively clean surface but suspect that one is there.

One option is to take a photograph of the area, wash down the area thoroughly, and then take a second photograph from exactly the same place as the first. When these photographs are fed into a computer,

FORENSIC DATA

THE KILLING OF KEVIN JACKSON

The significance of using impressions in a criminal investigation was shown when British police used tool specialists to help them track down the killers of 31-year-old Kevin Jackson. He had been stabbed in the head with a screwdriver when he tried to prevent thieves stealing his father's car from their home in Yorkshire. He died two days later.

When police arrested 21-year-old Rashad Zaman a few days later, they found a screwdriver in the back of his car. Microscopic traces of blood inside joints of the handle matched Kevin's blood and a tool marks specialist confirmed that marks inside the lock of Kevin's father's car had been made by this same tool.

A toolmark is a negative impression – in this case the kinds of marks left by the screwdriver in the lock when the thieves were trying to gain access to the car. Even if DNA testing had proved inconclusive when matching the blood found on the screwdriver in this case, this tool could be linked to the car from the marks it left. Because no two tools are alike, they image analysis software can be used to remove extraneous background information (such as scratches on a wooden floor) and look for differences between the two photographs. These differences could be traces of the footprint.

Forensic investigators used this technique in Toronto, Canada, to search for a footprint on a shop counter after an assault by a young man. They revealed a print from a size 12 Converse sneaker. Faint though it was, the suspect had made his mark.

will not leave identical impressions. Obvious differences such as size, width and shape are things that set tools apart, but there are also minute differences which can be discovered when examining a tool microscopically that are made to tools through use, manufacturing, finishing or grinding.

These weren't the only impressions that yielded important evidence. The police also arrested two other suspects, 20-year-old Rangzaib Akhtar and 21-year-old Raees Khan. Among the items they took from their homes were a pair of boots, which turned out to be spattered with blood that matched Kevin Jackson's DNA profile. On top of this, footmarks at the crime scene matched these boots, and inside the boots police found skin flakes that matched Zaman's DNA profile and hairs that matched Khan. Police concluded that the boots probably belonged to Khan but had been worn occasionally by Zaman. Another set of footwear marks left in the snow at the scene matched a pair of Nike trainers found at Akhtar's house.

In this case the clinching evidence came from skin scrapings found under the dead man's nails. It matched Khan and the three were all given life sentences for murder.

MURDEROUS TEETHMARKS

Teethmarks left in partially eaten food or hard cheese occasionally show up at some crime scenes, opening a new avenue of investigation. Police solved a politically motivated case in Northern Ireland with the help of a dental professor's remarkably accurate prediction about a person who'd discarded a half-eaten apple.

One early summer morning, Billy Craig was working on his car outside his parent's house just south of Belfast, Northern Ireland. He looked up as his father returned home from work, just in time to see a man step out of the bushes and shoot his father dead. Billy shouted at the gunman, who turned and shot him as well. While investigating the murder, police recovered a half-eaten apple lying in the bushes that overlooked the home. After interviewing many people, police concluded that the attacker must have left it there.

They sent it to a dental professor at the London School of Dentistry for forensic examination, and were shocked by the details that came back in the report. The professor said that the teethmarks were very unusual – the teeth were very misaligned, with the top row crowded and overlapping, and the two central incisors set at a V-shaped angle. There was evidence that the eater had not been able to bring his front teeth together. From this he predicted that the person who made the teeth marks would have a long narrow face, a large nose and a high sloping forehead. In addition, the person would have a protruding lantern jaw and a high vault in his palate.

The dentist went on to surmise that this person would be tall, have respiratory problems, large hands and feet, and be thin.

When police arrested Tony Kelly, who was part of an IRA unit, while investigating an ambush in which three police officers had been shot dead, they realised they had a man who fitted this description in almost every detail. Further dental surveys concluded that he had indeed bitten the apple. Ammunition collected from this ambush also matched the bullets that had killed the Craigs. Kelly was tried and convicted of all five murders. The bitten apple had been a vital clue.

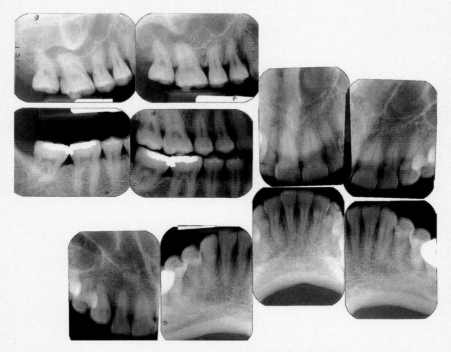

Accurate dental records, especially X-rays, such as the ones above, can be vital to an investigation since they can positively identify an individual. Teeth not only differ from person to person, but also last longer than other physical elements after death.

DOCUMENTS

Documents can be extremely useful in resolving a crime,
or the document itself may be the critical issue under
investigation. Whether handwritten or printed by
machine, or a combination of both, a document has a story
to tell that can be uncovered by an expert.

A document may be a ticket showing the time that a person crossed a toll
bridge. In one situation this could corroborate a suspect's alibi, while in
another it could indicate that he was near a crime scene at the relevant
time. A document examiner needs to consider whether there is any
evidence that the document had been forged or altered, and who had
created any handwriting on it, such as a signature.

HANDWRITTEN DOCUMENTS

From the moment a child picks up a pencil and starts scribbling, he or
she will begin to develop a unique way of holding and moving the pencil.
With increasing age, this turns into a unique handwriting style. We are,
after all, used to being able to recognise who has written us a letter just
from the handwriting on the envelope, and you can remember these
individual styles even when you only receive mail from someone once a
year – such as the aunt who sends you a birthday card.

Handwriting experts can take this widespread ability much further.
They can analyse a set of examples that they know were written by one
particular person, and then assess whether the same author penned the
text in a questioned document.

The expert looks for uniquely identifying features, such as:
• Variations in the slope of letters.
• Spacing between letters.
• Spacing between words.
• Indentations on the paper that show how hard the person pressed.
• Relative differences in letter heights.
• Where each letter begins and finishes.

The police may have found a letter and want evidence that a particular person wrote it. If they find a writing pad of similar paper in a suspect's house, they may have the evidence they need. When you write on one sheet of a pad, the pen often indents the sheet below. These indentations may be too slight for anyone to make sense of just by looking at them. But sprinkle fine particles of printer toner on it, place a plastic sheet on top, and then wave an electrostatic "wand" over it, and the toner will gather in the indentations. In one simple move you can go from a blank sheet to compelling evidence.

If the document is a booklet, each page should bear indentations from the page before. If this is not the case, there's a good chance that a page has been torn out, and analysing the indentations left on the remaining pages may reveal the missing text.

Signatures are an obvious target for forgers. The forger either traces the outline of a signature onto a document, fills it in with ink and then rubs out the tracing marks, or uses a light box to make the original signature visible on the new document and draws over that.

A big giveaway is that these signatures can look more belaboured than the original. Also, if more than one signature is needed on a set of documents, then an expert may notice they're all absolutely identical – something that wouldn't normally happen if the signatures were genuine.

MACHINE-WRITTEN DOCUMENTS

Typewriters and computer-linked printers give an initial impression of producing a very uniform script. But there is plenty of irregularity for a forensic expert to work on.

1. Any machine that uses keys to strike a character onto the paper is bound to have anomalies in one or more of its letters. An "o" may be partially filled in, or an "l" may have a partial break somewhere in the character. Checking two or more documents with a microscope could establish that they have come from the same machine.

2. Alternatively, looking at all the text in a single document may reveal that one word or numeral has been added by a different machine. A word like "not" could change a document's entire meaning; an added zero or two could alter the value of a bank cheque significantly, and evidence that a name has been erased can be detected under infrared light.

3. Few people these days still use typewriters, or daisywheel or golfball printers, but many documents that are important for forensic examinations are years old and were created with these machines. Anyone wanting to alter such documents will need to use one of these machines, or try to imitate its text by hand. A document examiner must therefore have a good understanding of these outdated printing methods.

4. Documents from laser and jet printers leave their mark in features such as the unique way the roller leaves indentations on the paper. Looking through a microscope at the way in which toner binds to the fibres in a sheet of paper gives vital clues about the type of printer used, and using

Examples of genuine Salvador Dali signatures, used to authenticate unknown pieces of the painter's work.

chromatography to break down the pigments can indicate what make of toner was in the printer. With experience, an expert can estimate the age of a document by assessing how much of the solvent used to carry the inks to the paper is present in the writing.

ASSESSING INKS

Whether a document is created by hand or by machine, analysing the ink could show that the writing was created using two different makes of pigment. This would immediately raise suspicions that the original document had been altered in some way.

The overall impression in natural light may be that ink used in a document is the same colour. A simple way to spot differences in ink is to take the document and shine on it a light source that consists of a very narrow band of wavelengths, such as infrared or ultraviolet light. Under such light sources, letters written with a different ink to the main part of the document stand out in a different colour to the rest, because pigments in the inks reflect different wavelengths. One crude test that is easy to perform is to hold a document under a regular yellow streetlight.

The white symbol (right) on this passport is only visible under untraviolet light and shows that the passport is genuine. The absence of this symbol is used to detect forgeries.

The sodium bulbs create monochromatic light and can sometimes reveal if different inks are present on the same page. On occasions, someone may have deliberately drawn over part of a document to hide the writing. Here handwriting experts use infrared light, which can penetrate the top layer of ink, and infrared-sensitive film, which may be able to detect what was written underneath. The technique will work only if the crossing out was done in type of ink that is significantly different to that used in creating the original text.

Infrared light and photography can also help decipher charred documents by increasing the contrast between the ink and the burned paper, and thus restoring the text.

IMAGE ANALYSIS

Forgers are becoming increasingly skilled at using high-quality scanners, software and computer printers to create fake documents. The range of possibility runs from counterfeit currency, to fake passports and forged bank bonds. This same computing power can, however, be turned to good use by forensic image experts in an effort to spot forgeries. With a scanner, a document examiner grabs a digitised image of a suspect document and feeds this information into a computer. Using image-analysis software, the expert alters the image's contrasts and colours. This shows up any anomalies that could indicate forgery.

Valuable documents often contain markings printed in inks that show up only when specific wavelengths of light are shone on them. The frequencies used are normally not present in normal daylight, but a scanner that can shine ultraviolet light on a document may be able to detect the hidden security features on genuine documents. Any that don't have these marks are shown to be fakes.

CURRENCY

Printing your own money is the fast way to riches. Over the years, central banks have gone to great lengths to make the task of the counterfeiter as

A forensic document examiner searches for minute details that may be a clue to the type of machine that was used to forge these passports.

hard as possible. For example, many banknotes incorporate such features as holograms and metal thread either woven through or printed onto the paper. The mints also attempt to make the forger's job as tricky as possible by choosing special papers and printed designs that are difficult to copy. Creating these anti-forging elements in currency is expensive, and if forgers tried to do it, the cost of creating the anti-forgery features on the currency would effectively remove the profit from their operation.

FORENSIC DATA

GILBERT V. CALIFORNIA, 1967

The *Gilbert v. California* case, heard by the California Supreme Court, set a couple of important precedents for cases involving handwriting analysis. The ways and means by which investigators gained access to a handwriting sample of the suspect was somewhat questionable, and in this case was influential in testing whether the handwriting sample could be admitted as evidence in court.

Gilbert had been arrested in Philadelphia on suspicion that he had been involved in a robbery. During the course of the robbery a handwritten note was used to demand a sum of money. While being interviewed by the FBI, Gilbert had given the investigating agent a sample of his handwriting, and this sample was used as evidence in court. The judge had to decide two important questions. First, had Gilbert's Fifth Amendment rights ruling out the use of self-incriminating evidence been violated? Second, should Gilbert's lawyer have been with him during the exemplar session?

In answer to the first question, the court said, "A mere handwriting exemplar, in contrast to the content of what is written, like the voice or body itself, is an identifying physical characteristic outside its protection." In other words, giving a handwriting exemplar does not provide self-incriminating evidence in violation of the Fifth Amendment. Answering the second, the court ruled that, "The taking of exemplars was not a 'critical' stage of the criminal proceedings entitling a petitioner to the assistance of counsel." Again, no violation occurs if a defendant gives an exemplar without his lawyer being present. The handwriting examplar became one of the most compelling pieces of evidence that led to Gilbert's conviction.

The watermark: the faint image similar to the large portrait, which is part of the paper itself and is visible from both sides when held up to the light.

Special, very high-quality rag paper with small red and blue threads throughout is used. It has a distinctive texture and color. The color-shifting ink images change color when the note is tinted.

The security thread: visible from both sides when held up to the light. This vertical strip of plastic is embedded in the paper.

Counterfeit features present on a US dollar bill. Even when the reproduction of a banknote looks perfect to the naked eye, simple ink absorption techniques can distinguish between genuine and forged notes.

When searching for fake banknotes, a scientist carefully checks each of these features. He or she also looks at the quality and texture of the paper itself. One quick test is to shine an ultraviolet light on a banknote, or draw a line on it with an iodine pen. These detect fluorescent brighteners and starch in the paper – materials that are not present in genuine notes.

INSIDE FORENSICS

COLLECTING SAMPLES OF WRITING

Some criminals try to disguise their handwriting to avoid revealing their identity. Some change the size of the letters and their slant, write in another person's handwriting style, or deliberately misspell words. Others may print in block capitals or write with their other hand.

As part of their work, handwriting experts must collect the right sort of "exemplar" samples – samples of writing that the forensic document examiner can use to check a person's normal style. These samples need to be written using the same sort of pencil or pen as had been used in the original evidence, and on the same sort of paper.

On occasions, documents such as letters to banks, employers or friends can be admitted as examples of a person's normal writing. The problem here is that, on the whole, no one has witnessed these letters being written, so the prosecution could have problems when it comes to presenting these as evidence if the case comes before a court. The way around this is to get the suspect to produce a piece of writing in front of witnesses. If the suspect is guilty, he or she may want to disguise their writing. To counter this possibility, the person is seated at a comfortable desk and has the original text dictated to them on three separate occasions. Each time the original is kept out of sight, as is any previous version. The person who is dictating gives no indication of spelling or punctuation. Unless the person is very practised, it will be difficult to regularly reproduce specific spelling errors, or features within the writing that break from the suspect's normal style. An expert may not be able to say what the person's true style is, but may come to the conclusion that the suspect has something to hide.

ELECTRONIC SLEUTHING

Section 3: page 134

- Voice Analysis
- Computer Analysis
- The Web

VOICE ANALYSIS

A suspect cassette tape arrives in the post at a newspaper office. The recorded voice claims to be that of a known terrorist and issues a warning. Is this a hoax or the real thing? The police become involved, and soon the tape is winging its way to a voiceprint expert.

The basic idea behind voice analysis is simple. Just as everyone has a unique fingerprint, they also have a unique voiceprint. By this, investigators mean that you can analyse the way that a person produces words to the extent that you can pinpoint who is speaking. Unlike fingerprints, however, the debate still rages in academic and forensic communities about how accurate any voiceprint assessment can be. On the other hand, there are now plenty of court cases that have turned on the basis of voiceprint evidence.

Voice analysis is increasingly being used in situations where investigators are attempting to track down a person who has made repeated malicious, threatening or obscene telephone calls. It can also provide useful leads where there are recordings of telephone calls made from the scene of a crime to the emergency services while a crime is taking place and the recordings pick up words not only from the victim but also from the assailants.

On top of this, voiceprint analysis has helped investigators on the (relatively rare) occasions when a murderer has telephoned the police to let them know the location of a body, or when after accidentally injuring someone (as in the case of a hit-and-run accident) and then fleeing from the scene, a person calls for an ambulance to attend the victim.

SOUNDING OUT SPECTROGRAPHS

A person generates words by creating vibrations in the air. These are shaped by the tension that he or she applies to the vocal cords in the throat, as well as how the muscles in the tongue and jaw contract and alter the shape of the space inside their mouth. The resulting sound is also influenced by the shape of anatomical features like the sinuses and the air passages in the nose.

As this anatomy varies considerably between people there is a natural variation in people's voices. Add to this the effect of education, social upbringing, national and regional environment, and age, and you have a huge number of variables that makes each person's voice distinct.

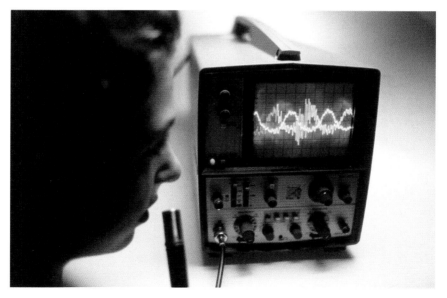

Sound waves produced during speech are converted into an electrical current and represented as a voiceprint on an oscilloscope.

FORENSIC DATA

THE DADDY OF VOICE ANALYSIS

AG Bell (1847-1922), the forerunner of voiceprinting techniques.

In 1882, Alexander Melville Bell published a book called *Visible Speech*, in which he showed a way of visually representing voice patterns. His method was limited to assessing the way people use punctuation, but he showed that even with this small part of the spoken word, he could distinguish different people. His son, Alexander Graham Bell, took the idea further. Initially motivated by the desire to help deaf people, he ended up using his inventions to develop the first telephones. Over half a century later, in 1941, the Bell Laboratories in New Jersey, US, produced a sound spectrograph that could map a voice onto paper, and slowly forensic scientists realised that they had a new weapon in their armoury.

Voiceprinting was first used in criminal investigations in the early 1960s by New York City police who were investigating bomb threats by telephone to major airlines. The technology took over two years to perfect and even longer before such evidence was admissible in court. Today when voiceprinting is used as evidence, certain precautions are observed to make sure it is given in context and properly understood by juries.

A light spectrograph splits a beam of light into the individual wave bands and then measures the intensity of each. So, too, a sound spectrograph splits a sound recording into different wavelengths and records the intensity of each. But with a sound spectrograph there is an added dimension – time. To make any sense of the complexities of speech, the sound spectrograph needs to record how the intensities of each wavelength of sound change over time. The result is a multicoloured chart that streams out as sound information is played. The horizontal axis of a voiceprint represents time, the vertical axis shows the frequency, and the degree of darkness within each region of the graph indicates the intensity of that frequency.

As is the case in working with handwriting, a forensic expert needs an authentic example to compare with a crime-related one. In voice analysis, the reference example takes the form of a tape recording of the person's voice as he or she speaks normally. The expert notes any differences between this and the crime-related tape, and works out if the two samples were made by the same person.

JUST LISTENING

As well as using the spectrograph, forensic experts who work in voice analysis learn to listen intently. We all know how easy it is to recognise the voice of people we know when they call us on the telephone. Very often the caller doesn't even need to announce their name before we know who they are. Voiceprint experts look to build on this type of unthinking skill.

The sorts of things voice analysts listen to are breath patterns, inflections, unusual speech habits and accents. They compare single sounds, as well as series of sounds, for similarities and discrepancies.

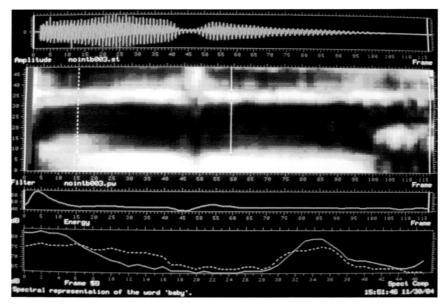

A computer graphics screen image of various waveform representations of the voiceprint for the word "baby", produced by a speech synthesiser.

BEING CERTAIN

Although voice analysis has been going on for more than a century, and voiceprints have been used in several cases in the UK and US to confirm the identity of telephone callers, forensic voice experts still debate quite how reliable the tests are. Voice analysts need to be well trained before they have a chance of persuading a judge and jury that their evidence is valid.

All the same, there's a growing consensus that if you find at least 20 key speech sounds that appear to be identical between a piece of taped voice evidence and a reference recording you can conclude that they match. Furthermore, the American Board of Recorded Evidence says that finding 15 matching sounds and no unexplained differences can be taken as a probable identification, while 10 sounds with no unexplained differences gives a possible identification.

Voiceprinting techniques can also be used to eliminate people from suspicion. Ten or more differences mean that the voice on the evidence tape is possibly not the person under suspicion; 15 or more non-matching sounds mean that they are probably not matched and 20 indicate that the two tapes come from different people.

FORENSIC DATA

VOICE OF A KILLER

Voiceprints became a critical part of the investigation into the murder of gamewarden Neil LaFeve. In 1971, police found his body after an extended search through the Wisconsin woods where he worked. He had been shot repeatedly in the head with a .22 rifle and then decapitated.

Investigators suspected that the assailant might have been a poacher, and started interviewing people who LaFeve had caught in the past. It wasn't long before 21-year-old Brian Hussong started to climb up the list of suspects. Police got permission to tap his phone. With the police listening, Hussong phoned his grandmother asking her to hide his guns and provide him with an alibi. In the phone call she seemed happy to cooperate, but police were soon on her doorstep to recover Hussong's gun.

When the case came to court, Hussong's grandmother denied saying that she would hide the gun. Voice experts showed that the voice in the taped phone call belonged to her, and that the other voice in the recording was Hussong's. Hussong was soon serving a life sentence in prison.

THE MOST INFAMOUS VOICE OF ALL

There surely can be no crime in the world that gained as much media attention as the suicide attacks on the Pentagon and the World Trade Center on September 11, 2001. And there can be few people in the world whose voice has been scrutinised as much as the terrorists' mastermind and paymaster, Osama bin Laden.

A month after the attacks, US forces invaded Afghanistan, targeting bin Laden and his Al-Qaida network there. The invasion crippled Al-Qaida, but bin Laden wasn't found. Is he alive or dead?

The possibility that bin Laden is still alive stems mainly from the regular appearance of videos and voice-tape messages that appear to include the voice of the man himself. These have been subjected to intense scrutiny as experts bring to bear all the techniques at their disposal to determine whether they really do come from him.

The first one arrived in December 2001. It was a poor-quality video recording with muffled sound and images that were at times blurred and jumpy. Most of the video showed only the side of the speaker's head, making it hard for voice experts to tell whether the sound and the images had been recorded at the same time, or whether the sound had been dubbed on top of an old recording. All the same, analysis of the voice, the words used, and phraseology convinced experts that the tape was genuine.

US experts pronounced genuine a tape released in October 2002. Swiss voice analysts disagreed, questioning the tape's authenticity.

وتية من أسامة بن لادن - زعيم تنظيم

Bin Laden's voice, aired on Al-Jazeera TV in a controversial 47-minute tape recording, highlighted the fact that voice analysis is still far from conclusive.

Whoever was right, the controversy highlights the fact that voice analysis has a long way to go before it can come up with definite conclusions.

Forensics experts said that a video recording released in September 2003, which showed Osama bin Laden walking in the Afghan mountains, appeared to have been filmed two years earlier, but they believed that the voice was bin Laden's and must have been recorded more recently, as it referred to recent political developments in the Middle East. Since then, two further video tapes, released in October 2003 and January 2004, had all the hallmarks of bin Laden's speech. This elusive character appears to be still on the run.

COMPUTER ANALYSIS

The phenomenal growth in computer use from the 1970s onward created a massive region of unguarded virtual real estate over which criminals could roam. All sorts of criminal activity is possible in this electronic realm, from conspiring to defraud a corporation to amassing child pornography.

Before the 1980s computers were large mainframe machines at the centre of large companies. It wasn't long before a few technicians with access to these machines realised that they could begin to defraud their employers.

FORENSIC DATA

THE ONE-HALF-CENT CRIME

A popular defrauding activity within the banking world has became known as the "one-half-cent crime". When a bank calculates the interest owed to a customer, it tracks the amount to the third decimal place or more. However, the bank ignores the fractional amount on any statement (but the amount is still held in the person's account). Unscrupulous computer operators came up with the idea to set up an account in their own name, and syphon off all these fractional cents. The beauty of the scam was that it was almost impossible to spot. In a small bank this created an income of some few hundred dollars a year, but in a larger one it could amass a few thousand dollars a month.

LEAVING A TRAIL OF DATA

A computer forensics expert's task is normally to gather information from a suspect's computer that will enable investigators to assess whether this information is evidence of a crime or a violation of company policy. An important source of information comes from pieces of data automatically gathered by a computer.

As computer use has grown, the number of occasions when we leave a trail of electronic evidence behind has exploded. For example:

The registry
At the heart of current Windows software is an area called the registry. The registry is a hidden database that stores information about the hardware plugged into the machine, as well as the software loaded on it.

Frauds such as these point to two key vulnerabilities of computer use:

1. Data is almost always invisible and is therefore very hard to keep track of. (This fact has advantages and disadvantages for computer forensics experts – it's difficult for authorities to stop some crimes, but it's equally difficult for criminals to cover their tracks because they can never be sure of erasing all aspects of their activities.)

2. Computer technology is a very fast-moving area, and one where the law is having difficulty keeping up. For example, until 1993 there were no laws in the United States defining computer crimes, and many of the newly created laws surrounding computer crime still have not been tested in court.

It also holds user preferences and set-up information. It's a fragile area of software, and people who don't know what they're doing should not tamper with it or they risk having to reformat their entire computer. But to a forensics expert the registry can be a goldmine. In it is information about the last person to use the machine, as well as the time it was used, which software packages were opened and which websites were visited.

The Internet browser software

This software lists website addresses and stores content of recently visited web pages. This has important legal ramifications, because it can provide evidence of when your computer was used to visit particular sites.

Cookies

Small files called cookies may be downloaded onto the computer from websites without the computer user's knowledge. Cookies are then used to hold information about the computer user or sometimes even to track them as they go from one site to another. Forensic examination of cookies is yet another way of noting how the machine has been used.

Seeing over partitions

Computer hard disks store vast masses of data. To help keep this data in sensible blocks so that you can find what you're looking for, software companies have built tools that throw partitions across the disk.

The files behind a partition remain in the computer, but a casual user of the machine won't know where to find them – they're effectively invisible. For a criminal, this represents a great way to hide incriminating information, whether it be on a company computer or a home one. Forensic computer experts use a software tool like Norton Disk Edit to look over the partition into the hidden storage space.

MAKING COPIES

It's a strange dichotomy that computer data seems almost indestructible, but is also fragile and easily altered. Computers may leave files ready for a computer expert to restore, but these are easily overwritten.

Just turning a computer on or off sets the machine opening a series of files, a process that influences the hard disk. This could destroy some of the evidence an expert is looking for or provide an opportunity for a good defence lawyer to instill doubt into jurors' minds by arguing that files were altered by the very act of examining the machine.

Seizing a computer

When investigators arrive to seize a suspect's computer, they will likely follow these procedures:

1. Officers will simply pull out the machine's power lead on arrival at a suspect's house and confiscate the hard disk.

2. Back at the lab, a copy of the hard disk is made. This is not a matter of simply copying over the files, because this would just move over the currently visible data, and leave any hidden or deleted files and file fragments behind. Using special analysis systems, computer experts perform a bit-stream download, in which they plug a suspect disk into another computer and make an absolute copy of the information in it.

3. Wherever possible, forensic examiners try to get hold of an identical disk to the one in the computer they are investigating. If that is not possible, the receiving disk needs to be at least as large, if not larger than the original evidence disk.

PROBLEMS OF PRIVACY

For any evidence to be useful to an investigation it needs to be admissible in court. Here there are some issues that have to be considered carefully, particularly in the US, where the Fourth Amendment to the Constitution safeguards a person's privacy. The Fourth Amendment generally prohibits law enforcement from accessing and viewing information stored in a computer without a warrant if it would be prohibited from opening a closed container, such as a briefcase or file cabinet, and examining its contents in the same situation. If forensic investigators seize a computer and examine the contents of its hard disk without gaining a search warrant, this could leave the prosecution open to the charge that the evidence is inadmissible because of a breach of privacy.

However, a landmark case in 1988 has changed things slightly. A defendant in a murder trial had stored incriminating evidence on his work-based computer. His attorney appealed to the Supreme Court in an attempt to prevent the prosecution from using the computer files as evidence because the investigators had failed to get a search warrant to access personal files on this work-based computer. The court ruled in favour of the prosecution, setting a precedent that a search warrant may not always be needed. Even so, getting a search warrant is preferable if police investigators want to give the evidence the maximum chance of being heard in court.

In the UK things go further, because the Regulation of Investigatory Powers Act 2000 makes it an offence not to hand over "keys" used to encrypt data if the data could be seen to be a threat to national security, could help prevent or detect crime, or would be in the interests of the economic well-being of the United Kingdom. British investigators have the weight of the law behind them.

FORENSIC DATA

JOHN POINDEXTER

Restoring files from a computer's hard disk is not the only possibility of securing evidence against someone suspected of a crime. One of the most high-profile cases of file restoration highlights another opportunity for forensic teams – backup copies.

Vice Admiral John M Poindexter had been appointed as president Reagan's national security adviser in December, 1985, but was forced to resign the following year after proof of his involvement in supplying Iran with arms – the so-called Iran/Contra affair. This operation involved two Reagan Administration policies, involving the national security staff. Through 1985 and 1986, weapons were sold to Iran to secure the release of American hostages in the Middle East, despite the fact that the US Congress had forbidden such actions.

President Reagan asserted that he had not been "fully informed" about some details of the Iran operation and two high-ranking officials, Colonel Oliver North and John Poindexter, were relieved of their duties after "serious questions of propriety had been raised".

Poindexter repeatedly lied to Congress about his role in helping the Contras, and he and others worked hard to erase thousands of computer files and shred paper evidence of their dealings. However, when forensics experts examined White House backup tapes they revealed more than 5,000 messages, which when added together allowed investigators to discover much of what had gone on.

In 1988 John Poindexter was indicted for defrauding the United States government and obstructing justice. He was convicted in 1990 and sentenced to serve time in prison.

NOT SO DELETED

A man with images of child pornography on his computer deletes the images before police move in. Confident the files are erased, he tells detectives that he's got nothing to hide.

Forensic computer experts know better. When a person deletes a file, the computer is lazy. Instead of erasing all the information, it just overwrites the initial character from the title line that the computer uses to identify a file. This tells the computer that the following area is unallocated disk space and can be overwritten. With appropriate analytical software, forensic computer experts can search for files with broken labels, rebuild the label and open the file.

The only problem for forensic examiners is that once a file is "deleted" the space on the disk becomes available for the computer to overwrite it with a new file. If this has happened, the information may be lost. But there are ways around that problem, too. When a computer saves a large file, it often breaks it into smaller chunks and spreads them around the disk. It may be that the computer has overwritten one or more of the small regions, but a forensic computer expert can salvage enough from the areas that haven't been destroyed to retrieve the evidence they are after. A deleted and overwritten file of an image of child pornography could be reconstructed to a sufficient extent to incriminate the computer's owner. Even if the data has been overwritten a number of times it's sometimes possible to recover the data by measuring the small magnetic differences still present on the disk.

All computer systems, including electronic diaries, leave some kind of trail. As long ago as 1986 drug smuggler Paul Dye was convicted in the UK on the basis of files apparently deleted but recovered from a Psion electronic diary. Forensics experts had to get the Psion corporation to build the appropriate tools, but it was possible to do.

Paul Gadd, AKA Gary Glitter, the Seventies glamrock legend who fell from grace in 1997 when he was arrested and accused of downloading child pornography from the Internet. In November 1999, Gadd was sentenced to four months in prison and since then has also been detained and then deported from his new residence in Cambodia over allegations of sex offences against young boys. He remains on the UK Sex Offenders' Register.

THE WEB

Massive computer networks now extend around the globe so that at little cost we can send messages to far-flung places and access files held on distant computers, all at the click of a computer mouse. The network of computers, satellites and cables is the Internet, and the software systems that make it easy to use make up the World Wide Web. Since the early 1990s the Internet and the web have developed at such a pace that they have changed the way that many people live, do business – and commit crime.

The problem that investigators and legislators face with Internet-based crime stems from the system's initial design concept. When the system that became the Internet was first developed in the US during the Cold War, the aim was to create a communication system that would be impossible to block even if half the country had been devastated by a nuclear attack. The result was a network of computers that has no central controlling facility, and will automatically search for new ways of linking two places if the normal channels are broken. Nowadays, the Internet reaches to most corners of the world. It's quite possible for someone in a developing country to sit in a shack on the edge of a slum with a laptop computer and phone line, and release viruses that bring mighty corporations grinding to a halt on the other side of the globe. Or people can hack into computer databases and steal or alter data, causing massive disruption without even entering the country where the data is held.

The pace of change in this area is incredible and forensic computer experts and large corporations need to keep up with it. One of the areas

Germany, 2003: A forensics investigator displays evidence confiscated during an enquiry into an international on-line child pornography ring.

of most concern is hacking, the illegal accessing of a computer system. The US Department of Homeland Security recorded 702,357 hacking incidents in December 2003, an increase from 30,000 for December 2002 and only 4,901 for December 2001. There's clearly plenty of work for a forensic scientist who wants to specialise in this area.

A HACKER ATTACKS

Hacking comes in many different forms:

🖰 Someone trying to quietly gain access to confidential information on a website, hoping to make use of it without being spotted.

🖰 Someone wanting to overwrite a company website with propaganda designed to damage or embarrass the company.

🖰 Someone who creates a website that resembles a large corporation's site, the aim being to gain clients' confidential details, including credit card information.

The procedure

1. The first responder in such cases is usually someone in the corporation's IT department.

2. He or she first determines if the hacker is still working within the system, or whether the attack has finished. If it's ongoing, the system may be closed to prevent further damage. But there's a dilemma – the best option is to do as little as possible, so that you don't inadvertently erase anything that investigators might be able to use to track down the hacker.

3. Everything possible is documented. Names, times and events are jotted down, and screenshots and digital pictures taken. All of this data will help investigators at a later stage.

4. If appropriate, photographs are taken of the office where suspect computers are housed. This records the location of machines, chairs and people during the incident. It could be, for example, that a hacker is part of the office team.

TRACKING THE HACKER

By definition, hackers are people who thoroughly understand the inner workings of computers and the Internet, and are therefore in a prime position to cover their tracks. They could also be operating from anywhere in the world, making the chance of arresting them more remote than is the case in other physical crimes.

Consequently, most organisations decide simply to close the holes in their software as quickly as possible when they find it's been hacked

In May 2000, the Lovebug virus was unleashed and clogged computers worldwide. The FBI traced the source to an apartment in Makati City, Philippines, but this is where the forensic trail ended, as they were unable to press charges on any of the residents.

into, and carry on with their work. If the company in question decides to pursue an attacker, they first need to search for relevant data that will shed light on which company gave the hacker access to the Internet. When computers link together over the Internet, they swap sets of numbers referred to as IP addresses. These are groups of four numbers separated by three dots, and can be traced back to the original source. If you can find the hacker's IP address then you are on the trail. Unfortunately, this is less useful than it may seem, because hackers often use methods that hide their true identity – often by the hacker using an innocent PC that's been loaded with rogue software – and the evidence trail soon runs cold. If a computer has been hacked, forensic computer experts make it a rule not to use any software tools that are currently installed on that machine. This is because the hacker may have overwritten these tools with versions that have been altered so that they deliberately turn a blind eye to hacking activities. All analytical software tools are freshly installed or run from a separate machine.

Often the next step is to combine this forensic search with good old-fashioned, on-foot detective work. Information found on a computer hard disk may lead investigators to a particular community – either on-line or physical, or both – and then local information can point the finger of suspicion at particular individuals. In the world of cybercrime, whether police can secure a conviction or not, is another matter.

FORENSIC DATA

HACKING INTO NASA

Twenty-year-old Jason Diekman of Orange County, California, was arrested after suspicious officials started to tap his telephone line and heard him discussing how to commit credit card frauds.

It transpired that over the previous two years Diekman had illegally accessed government computers at NASA's Jet Propulsion Laboratory in Pasadena, NASA computers at Stanford University and numerous other government and university computer systems. His access was so extensive that he could often control all aspects of the computers, including the ability to modify files and alter security on the systems. This appears to have been just the tip of the iceberg, as Deikman claims to have hacked thousands of computers around the world. On February 4, 2002, Diekman was sentenced to 21 months in federal prison, three years' supervised release, restricted use of the computer and over $87,000 in restitution.

GLOSSARY

acquittal: to be released from custody when found not guilty of a crime.

alibi: a defense given by the accused that he was elsewhere when a crime was committed.

amphetamines: a group of drugs used medically to combat fatigue and illicitly as a mood-enhancing stimulant.

antibody: a molecule used by animals to fend off infections.

arson: deliberately setting property on fire and causing criminal damage.

automatic weapon: a firearm that uses the explosive force of one round of ammunition to mechanically load the next round and set the gun ready to fire again.

autopsy: an examination of a human body that attempts to discover how the person died.

ballistics: the scientific study of how bullets and other projectiles travel through the air.

blood spatter patterns: characteristic shapes of blood marks that give information about how the blood was shed.

chain of custody: a record of who has examined a piece of forensic evidence from the moment that it was discovered.

chloroform: a solvent that is used to dissolve many materials that can't be dissolved in water.

chromatography: a range of techniques that break chemical samples down into their constituent parts.

class physical evidence: a piece of evidence that belongs to a distinct category of items, such as a cigarette belonging to a known brand.

CODIS: Combined DNA Index System used by the FBI to store genetic fingerprints so that suspects can be rapidly linked to evidence from other crime scenes.

comparison microscope: two microscopes coupled together so that the scientist can compare two separate pieces of evidence simultaneously.

counterfeit: an imitation or copy of a valuable object or document.

cyanoacrylic: the chemical in a group of glues that bind firmly to the amino acids, fatty acids and proteins found in fingerprints.

defendant: a person accused of a crime.

Deoxyribonucleic acid (DNA): the information-carrying molecule in the centre of cells.

electrophoresis: a method for separating chemicals within a sample that make use of the fact that different chemical molecules are different sizes and carry differing electrical charges.

enzyme: biological molecule that increases the rate of a specific chemical reaction.

evidence: any item that throws light on a crime.

exemplar: a sample of handwriting that is known to come from a particular individual and can be used to compare writing found on pieces of evidence.

expert witness: someone asked by a court to give evidence because they have particular skills or experience that can help the judge and jury understand aspects of a trial.

eyewitness: a person who saw an event and can recount what they think occurred.

fingerprints: the highly individual set of marks left by a person's fingers when he or she touches or picks up an object.

firearms: any weapon that fires bullets or shot.

forensic: any work that relates to legal matters.

genetic fingerprinting: a way of analysing a person's DNA that produces a record that is specific to that individual.

hacker: a person who deliberately accesses private information held on a computer.

illicit drug: a drug that is used without legal permission.

impressed print: a mark, such as a fingerprint or footmark, that has created an indentation in the surface of a piece of evidence.

individual evidence: evidence that can be linked with a high degree of certainty to a specific item or person.

latent print: marks that can only be detected when exposed with a chemical dye or powder.

LSD: a potent drug that triggers hallucinations and altered memory.

luminol: a chemical that reacts with iron found in blood cells to emit a blue light.

mass spectrometer: a machine that breaks molecules into fragments and then tells you the mass of each fragment.

neutron activation analysis: a technically complex method of chemical analysis that determines what chemical elements are present in a sample.

patent prints: clearly visible prints or marks left by other parts of the body or clothing.

pathology: the branch of medicine that diagnoses disease and causes of death, by analysing body fluids and examining samples of cells and tissues.

psychiatry: the branch of medicine that deals with mental illness and personality disorders.

physical evidence: any item that helps investigators discover what occurred at a crime scene.

poison: a chemical that causes severe harm to living organisms.

polymerase chain reaction: a set of chemical reactions that can increase the amount of a genetic sample and yield enough genetic material for scientists to analyse.

psychology: the scientific study of human behaviour.

reconstruction: using actors to recreate the events that lead up to a crime.

rifle: a firearm that has a spiraling set of grooves cut into the inside of the barrel that makes the bullet spin as it flies through the air.

rigor mortis: tension in muscles that occurs soon after a person has died.

scanning electron microscope: a machine that generates detailed 3-D photographs of microscopically small items. It can magnify an object by about 100,000 times.

serology: the scientific study of body fluids including blood, saliva, sweat and semen.

shotgun: a firearm that discharges a mass of small pellets (shot) rather than a single bullet.

spectrophotometer: a scientific instrument that uses light to analyse purified samples taken from pieces of evidence and indicate what chemical is present.

toxicology: the study of chemicals that have harmful effects on living organisms.

Trojan: a computer program that has a hidden sinister capability.

voiceprint: the profile of an individual's voice used for matching purposes against another voice profile in an attempt to link it to that individual.

X-ray diffraction: a method used to determine the chemical composition of a sample.

INDEX